MY FAVOURITE STORIES
OF IRELAND

My Favourite STORIES OF Ireland

edited by
BRÍD MAHON

with line decorations by
PETER McCLURE

LUTTERWORTH PRESS
GUILDFORD AND LONDON

Printed in Great Britain by
Cox & Wyman Ltd
London, Fakenham and Reading

Acknowledgements

The editor and the publishers are indebted to all those who have given permission for the use of material which is their copyright, or have helped in the obtaining of that permission:

A. P. Watt & Son, for 'The Last Gleeman', taken from *Celtic Twilight* by W. B. Yeats

George Allen & Unwin (Publishers) Ltd, for 'The Aran Islands', abridged from their edition of the book of the same name by J. M. Synge

John Farquharson Ltd, for 'The Pug-Nosed Fox', taken from *Some Experiences of an Irish R.M.* by Somerville & Ross

Mrs Iris Wise, Macmillan of London and Basingstoke, and the Macmillan Company of Canada, for 'In the Wood of Coilla Doraca', taken from *The Crock of Gold* by James Stephens

The Longman Group Limited, for 'Never No More', taken from the book of the same name by Maura Laverty

Martin Brian & O'Keeffe Limited, for 'Poet', taken from *The Green Fool* by Patrick Kavanagh, © Katherine B. Kavanagh

Folens & Co. Ltd, for 'The Mysterious Beggarman', taken from *The Wonder Tales of Ireland* by Bríd Mahon

Constable & Company Limited, for 'Golden Stockings You Had On', taken from *The Collected Poems of Oliver St John Gogarty*

Liam O'Flaherty and Jonathan Cape Ltd, for 'The Wounded Cormorant', taken from *The Short Stories of Liam O'Flaherty*

A. D. Peters & Co. Ltd, for 'Weep For Our Pride', taken from *The Trusting and the Maimed* by James Plunkett

The literary estate of Maurice O'Sullivan, and Chatto and Windus Ltd, for 'The Whale', taken from *Twenty Years A-Growing* by Maurice O'Sullivan

Kevin Danaher, for 'At the Foot of the Rainbow', taken from his book *Gentle Places and Simple Things*

Contents

CONTENTS

Introduction

Ireland's greatest poet, William Butler Yeats, exhorted his fellow scribes to learn their trade so that

> *'We in coming days may be*
> *Still the indomitable Irishry.'*

But the Irishman wears a cloak of many colours, for from pre-historic times it has been our fate to play host—however un-willingly at times—to many peoples. Successive waves have come to our shores. Stone Age men, overtaken in time by men of the Bronze Age, and later tamed by men with iron swords. Early Celtic peoples whose voices we hear in our ancient legends and sagas. They were kings and warriors, farmers and raiders, who brought back with them booty and slaves like the boy Patrick who was later to Christianise the land.

The centuries passed, and the Vikings came in their long-prowed vessels. We recapture the feeling of the age in the writings of an unknown monk. Over a thousand years ago he noted hurriedly in the margin of his manuscript:

> *'The bitter wind is high tonight,*
> *It lifts the white locks of the sea.*
> *In such wild winter storm no fright*
> *Of savage Viking troubles me.'*

The Viking pirates were followed by traders and merchants who made of Dublin a Danish city, which in part it remains today. Perhaps the magnet that drew so many was the fact that until Columbus (or someone else) discovered the American continent, Ireland stood at the edge of the known world. The Danes were followed in time by Norman lords who built tall castles, and later still came swaggering Elizabethan adventurers, and after them grim-faced Cromwellian soldiers and Williamite planters and Huguenot refugees. The warp and woof of their various strands of culture were woven together to form a pattern which would inspire many of our writers. For indeed we are a nation of story-tellers and there is some truth in the claim that half of the great writers of English literature were Irishmen.

When I was first asked to edit this book, my difficulty was not in choosing my favourite writers, but rather a question of whom I would omit. A selection of my favourites would fill several volumes and the fact that I have not included writings from Joyce, Frank O'Connor, Sean O'Faolain, Mary Lavin, Edna O'Brien, Eilis Dillon, Walter Macken and a dozen more is a cause for regret—except that their works are to be found in almost every anthology of Irish writing to date.

What I have set out to do is to include a cross-section of Irish writers, covering a period of more than two hundred years and representing every walk of life. Many of the writers I have included have written their final word, but happily not all.

My first choice was William Butler Yeats, who was born in Sandymount, Dublin, where I live. Generations of my forbears came from the Liberties of Dublin, and as a child on my way to school I frequently stopped in Black Pitts to buy a bag of home-made treacle toffee in a little shop where Zosimus was said to have been born. Zosimus was the 'Last Gleeman of Dublin', and Yeats wrote an account of his life in a collection of essays called *The Celtic Twilight*. It was shortly after this that Yeats wrote his best-known poem, *The Lake Isle of Innisfree*, and fell in love with the legendary Maud Gonne, the inspiration for his love poems. When I was a small child I met Maud Gonne. Even in old age she was still 'a woman Homer sung'.

John Millington Synge, like Yeats, was of Ascendancy stock, and became the greatest dramatist of his day. In 1894 he settled in France and soon after he met Yeats, who said: 'Give up Paris, you will never create anything by reading Racine . . . Go to the Aran Islands. Live there as if you were one of the people themselves, express a life that has never found expression.' Synge paid his visit to Aran equipped with a notebook, a fiddle, and a Gaelic dic-

tionary, and subsequently wrote not only an account of life on the
Aran Islands, but also two of his greatest plays, *The Playboy
of the Western World* and *In the Shadow of the Glen*. An old
story-teller on Aran told him the stories from which he wove
the plays.

If Synge wrote of a group of islands where life had stood still
since medieval times, Somerville and Ross wrote of a world apart.
Their *genre* was the Ascendancy tradition from which they had
sprung, two girl cousins who early in life formed a literary partner-
ship. The incomparable *Experiences of an Irish R. M.* is their best-
known work and their portrayal of Ireland is no less true for being
the Ireland of the Big House and the Fox Hunt.

When the stories and sayings of a writer are woven into the
folklore of a people, it is proof of the impact the writer has made
on the Irish consciousness and imagination. Legends abound to this
day of Jonathan Swift, the enigmatic genius who walked the
cobbled streets of old Dublin and who reigned in the Deanery of
St Patrick's Cathedral more than two hundred years ago. In the
pulpit he violently denounced the beggars whose rags were the
tools of their trade, and yet he watered his wine, and walked
instead of using a coach, to save money to give them alms. No one
ever knew the true story of his stormy love affairs with 'Stella' and
'Vanessa', and none dared ask. He professed to hate and despise
Ireland, and yet risked reputation and imprisonment by writing in
her defence and making known her wrongs. *Gulliver's Travels* is
his most famous work, so timeless is it that the adventures told
might have been the creation of a modern-day science-fiction
writer.

After Swift, Oliver Goldsmith was the greatest writer of his age.
Born in 1728 of Anglo-Irish stock, educated at Trinity College,
like many writers he soon shook the dust of Ireland from his shoes.
He travelled on the Continent, and finally settled in London,
shabby, self-conscious from the scars of smallpox which disfigured
his face from childhood. His native village in County Westmeath
was the inspiration for his most famous poem, 'Sweet Auburn'
(*The Deserted Village*). I have included in this collection his *Elegy on
the Death of a Mad Dog*, at a special request of my nephews,
Stephen and Conor.

Once, long ago, I had the good fortune to meet James Stephens,
a little man who looked like a leprechaun, could crack his fingers,
tell stories as he wrote them, and once stood on his head for half an

hour at a party. *The Crock of Gold*, from which I include the first chapter, is my favourite book.

Maura Laverty was a close friend of mine until her death some years ago. Sean O'Faolain said of her book *Never No More* that it was a case of 'love at first sight'. Brendan Behan said there never was a book like it. It is Maura's own story of her girlhood in a little, lost village on the edge of the great Bog of Allen, and my inclusion of a chapter from the book is my tribute to her.

The poet Patrick Kavanagh was another friend of mine, and for a brief period he declared he was in love with me, 'only', as he said, he was 'too poor to marry'. (Later, he had a brief, happy marriage before his early death.) In London he was befriended by Helen Waddell, the writer and classical scholar, who encouraged him to write his first book, an autobiography, *The Green Fool*, from which I have taken the chapter 'Poet'. My last meeting with him was at a race-meeting, where he shared his sandwiches with me and gave me a winner.

Golden Stockings is an enchanting poem which Oliver St John Gogarty wrote for his little daughter Brenda. In his day he was Dublin's best-known surgeon, poet, senator and wit. He was also a one-time friend of James Joyce, who immortalized him as Buck Mulligan in *Ulysses*. (It is said that Gogarty was furious and never forgave Joyce.)

Sheridan Le Fanu was born in Dublin in 1814 of Anglo-Irish stock: a grand-nephew of the famous Irish dramatist Richard Brinsley Sheridan. *Uncle Silas*, a romance of terror, is probably his best-known work. The writer Elizabeth Bowen described it as 'an Irish story in an English setting'.

And with these, four short stories: Oscar Wilde's *The Happy Prince*; Liam O'Flaherty's *The Wounded Cormorant*; James Plunkett's *Weep for our Pride*, a vivid portrayal of school life in Dublin in the hungry thirties; and *The Mysterious Beggarman*, one of our best-loved legends.

Maurice O'Sullivan spent his youth on the Blasket Islands and wrote of his life there in *Twenty Years A-Growing*. From this book I have included a chapter called 'The Whale'. The Great Blasket, on the south-west corner of Ireland, was once said to be 'the next parish to America'. The Islanders were Irish-speaking with their own customs and traditions, and they produced some of the best story-tellers and writers in the Irish language. Now, alas, the

Blaskets are deserted, and the life that the islanders once lived but a story-book memory.

My final offering is from Kevin Danaher's *Gentle Place and Simple Things*, a step back into the Ireland of the nineteenth century, in which he recounts anecdotes and stories of highwaymen and ghosts, water-monsters and fairy forts, Norman keeps and thatched cottages. He is a colleague of mine in the Department of Irish Folklore at University College, Dublin, and a man of many parts. The chapter I have chosen, *At the Foot of the Rainbow*, tells of treasure trove—some found, some still waiting to be claimed: proof, if such is needed, that some of the stories Irish people tell happen to be true.

Bríd Mahon

To
R. and T. P. H.

I

The Last Gleeman

W. B. YEATS

Michael Moran was born about 1794 off Black Pitts, in the Liberties of Dublin, in Faddle Alley. A fortnight after birth he went stone blind from illness, and became thereby a blessing to his parents, who were soon able to send him to rhyme and beg at street corners and at the bridges over the Liffey. They may well have wished that their quiver were full of such as he, for, free from the interruption of sight, his mind became a perfect echoing chamber, where every movement of the day and every change of public passion whispered itself into rhyme or quaint saying. By the time he had grown to manhood he was the admitted rector of all the ballad-mongers of the Liberties. Madden the weaver, Kearney the blind fiddler from Wicklow, Martin from Meath, M'Bride from heaven knows where, and that M'Grane who in after days, when the true Moran was no more, strutted in borrowed plumes, or rather in borrowed rags, and gave out that there had never been any Moran but himself, and many another, did homage before him, and held him chief of all their tribe.

Nor despite his blindness did he find any difficulty in getting a wife, but rather was able to pick and choose, for he was just that mixture of ragamuffin and of genius which is dear to the heart of woman, who, perhaps because she is wholly conventional herself, loves the unexpected, the crooked, the bewildering. Nor did he lack despite his rags many excellent things, for it is remembered that he ever loved caper sauce, going so far indeed in his honest indignation at its absence upon one occasion as to fling a leg of mutton at his wife. He was not, however, much to look at, with his coarse frieze coat with its cape and scalloped edge, his old corduroy trousers and great brogues, and his stout stick made fast to his wrist by a thong of leather: and he would have been a woeful shock to the gleeman Mac Conglinne* could that friend of kings have beheld him in prophetic vision from the pillar stone at Cork. And yet though the short cloak and the leather wallet were no more, he was a true gleeman, being alike poet, jester, and newsman of the people.

In the morning when he had finished his breakfast, his wife or some neighbour would read the newspaper to him, and read on and on until he interrupted with, 'That'll do—I have me meditations': and from these meditations would come the day's store of jest and rhyme. He had the whole Middle Ages under his frieze coat.

He had not, however, Mac Conglinne's hatred of the Church and clergy, for when the fruit of his meditations did not ripen well, or when the crowd called for something more solid, he would recite or sing a metrical tale or ballad of saint or martyr or of Biblical adventure. He would stand at a street corner, and when a crowd had gathered would begin in some such fashion as follows (I copy the record of one who knew him)—'Gather round me, boys, gather round me. Boys, am I standin' in puddle? Am I standin' in wet?' Thereupon several boys would cry 'Ah, no! yez not! yer in a nice dry place. Go on with *St Mary*: go on with *Moses*'—each calling for his favourite tale. Then Moran with a suspicious wriggle of his body and a clutch at his rags, would burst out with 'All me buzzim friends are turned backbiters'; and after a final 'If yez don't drop your coddin' and deversion I'll lave some of yez a case', by way of warning to the boys, begin his recitation, or perhaps still delay, to ask 'Is there a crowd around me now? Any blackguard heretic around me?' The best-known of his religious tales was *St Mary of Egypt*, a long poem of exceeding solemnity, condensed from the much longer work of a certain Bishop Coyle. It told how a fast woman of Egypt, Mary by name,

* Mac Conglinne was a medieval Irish poet who fell foul of the monks of Cork but redeemed himself by relating a vision he had of a land of plenty. He won fame and fortune by curing the King of Munster of the demon of gluttony.

followed pilgrims to Jerusalem for no good purpose, and then turning penitent on finding herself withheld from entering the Temple by supernatural interference, fled to the desert and spent the remainder of her life in solitary penance. When at last she was at the point of death, God sent Bishop Zosimus to hear her confession, give her the last sacrament, and with the help of a lion, whom He sent also, dig her grave. The poem has the intolerable cadence of the eighteenth century, but was so popular and so often called for that Moran was soon nicknamed Zosimus, and by that name is he remembered.

He had also a poem of his own called *Moses*, which went a little nearer poetry without going very near. But he could ill brook solemnity, and before long parodied his own verses in the following ragamuffin fashion:

In Egypt's land, contagious to the Nile
King Pharaoh's daughter went to bathe in style
She tuk her dip, then walked unto the land
To dry her royal pelt she ran along the strand
A bulrush tripped her, whereupon she saw
A smiling babby in a wad o' straw
She tuk it up, and said with accents mild
'Tare-and-agers, girls, which av yez owns the child?'

His humorous rhymes were, however, more often quips and cranks at the expense of his contemporaries. It was his delight, for instance, to remind a certain shoemaker, noted alike for display of wealth and for personal uncleanness, of his inconsiderable origin in a song of which but the first stanza has come down to us:

At the dirty end of Dirty Lane
Liv'd a dirty cobbler, Dick Maclane
His wife was in the old king's reign
   A stout brave orange-woman
On Essex Bridge she strained her throat
And six-a-penny was her note
But Dikey wore a bran-new-coat
   He got among the yeomen.

He was a bigot, like his clan
And in the streets he wildly sang,
O Roly, toly, toly raid, with his old jade ——

He had troubles of divers kinds, and numerous interlopers to face and put down. Once an officious peeler arrested him as a vagabond but was triumphantly routed amid the laughter of the court, when Moran reminded His Worship of the precedent set by Homer who was also, he declared, a poet, and a blind man, and a beggarman. He had to face a more serious difficulty as his fame grew. Various imitators started up upon all sides. A certain actor, for instance, made as many guineas as Moran did shillings by mimicking his sayings and his songs and his get-up upon the stage. One night this actor was at supper with some friends, when dispute arose as to whether his mimicry was overdone or not. It was agreed to settle it by an appeal to the mob. A forty-shilling supper at a famous coffee-house was to be the wager. The actor took up his station at Essex Bridge, a great haunt of Moran's, and soon gathered a small crowd. He had scarce got through 'In Egypt's land, contagious to the Nile', when Moran himself came up, followed by another crowd. The crowds met in great excitement and laughter.

'Good Christians,' cried the pretender, 'is it possible that any man would mock the poor dark man like that?'

'Who's that? It's some imposhterer,' replied Moran.

'Begone, you wretch! it's you'ze the imposhterer. Don't you fear the light of heaven being struck from your eyes for mocking the poor dark man?'

'Saints and angels, is there no protection against this? You're a most inhuman blaguard to try to deprive me of my honest bread this way,' replied poor Moran.

'And you, you wretch, won't let me go on with the beautiful poem. Christian people, in your charity won't you beat this man away? He's taking advantage of my darkness.'

The pretender, seeing that he was having the best of it, thanked the people for their sympathy and protection, and went on with the poem, Moran listening for a time in bewildered silence. After a while Moran protested again with:

'Is it possible that none of yez can know me? Don't yez see it's myself; and that's some one else?'

'Before I proceed any further in this lovely story,' interrupted the pretender, 'I call on yez to contribute your charitable donations to help me to go on.'

'Have you no sowl to be saved, you mocker of heaven?' cried Moran, put completely beside himself by this last injury. 'Would

you rob the poor as well as desave the world? O, was ever such
wickedness known?'

'I leave it to yourselves, my friends,' said the pretender, 'to give
to the real dark man, that you all know so well, and save me from
that schemer,' and with that he collected some pennies and half-
pence. While he was doing so, Moran started his *Mary of Egypt*,
but the indignant crowd seizing his stick were about to belabour
him, when they fell back bewildered anew by his close resemblance to himself. The pretender now called to them to 'just give
him a grip of that villain, and he'd soon let him know who the
imposhterer was'! They led him over to Moran but instead of
closing with him he thrust a few shillings into his hand, and turning to the crowd explained to them he was indeed but an actor,
and that he had just gained a wager, and so departed amid much
enthusiasm, to eat the supper he had won.

In April 1846 word was sent to the priest that Michael Moran
was dying. He found him at 15 (now 14½) Patrick Street, on a
straw-bed in a room full of ragged ballad-singers come to cheer
his last moments. After his death the ballad-singers, with many
fiddles and the like, came again and gave him a fine wake, each
adding to the merriment whatever he knew in the way of rann,
tale, old saw or quaint rhyme. He had had his day, had said his
prayers and made his confession, and why should they not give
him a hearty send-off?

The funeral took place the next day. A good party of his
admirers and friends got into the hearse with the coffin, for the
day was wet and nasty. They had not gone far when one of them
burst out with 'It's cruel cowld, isn't it?'

'Garra,' replied another, 'we'll all be as stiff as the corpse when
we get to the berrin-ground.'

'Bad cess to him,' said a third; 'I wish he'd held out another
month until the weather got dacent.'

A man called Carrol thereupon produced a half-pint of whiskey,
and they all drank to the soul of the departed. Unhappily, however, the hearse was over-weighted, and they had not reached the
cemetery before the spring broke, and the bottle with it.

Moran must have felt strange and out of place in that other
kingdom he was entering, perhaps while his friends were drinking
in his honour. Let us hope that some kindly middle region was
found for him, where he can call dishevelled angels about him
with some new and more rhythmical form of his old

Gather round me, boys, will yez
Gather round me?
And hear what I have to say
Before ould Salley brings me
My bread and jug of tay ——

and fling outrageous quips and cranks at cherubim and seraphim.
Perhaps he may have found and gathered, ragamuffin though he
be, the Lily of High Truth, the Rose of Far-sight Beauty, for
whose lack so many of the writers of Ireland, whether famous or
forgotten, have been futile as the blown froth upon the shore.

st Attracta slays the monster

2

The Aran Islands

J. M. SYNGE

Three islands, Aranmore, Inishmaan and Inishere, make up the group known as the Aran Islands, on the western seaboard of Ireland. The islanders, a close-knit community of fishing folk and small farmers, are famous for many things, notably story-telling, hand-knitted Aran sweaters, and a film called Man of Aran *which was made many years ago. Synge's visit was made over eighty years ago, at the suggestion of W. B. Yeats. His account is here slightly abridged:*

I am settled at last on Inishmaan in a small cottage with a continual drone of Gaelic coming from the kitchen that opens into my room.

Early this morning the man of the house came over for me with a four-oared curagh—that is, a curagh with four rowers and four oars on either side, as each man uses two—and we set off a little before noon.

It gave me a moment of exquisite satisfaction to find myself moving away from civilization in this rude canvas canoe of a model that has served primitive races since men first went on the sea.

We had to stop for a moment at a hulk that is anchored in the bay, to make some arrangements for the fish-curing of the middle island, and my crew called out as soon as we were within earshot that they had a man with them who had been in France a month from this day.

When we started again, a small sail was run up in the bow, and we set off across the Sound with a leaping oscillation that had no resemblance to the heavy movement of a boat.

The sail is only used as an aid, so the men continued to row after it had gone up, and as they occupied the four cross-seats I lay on the canvas at the stern and the frame of slender laths, which bent and quivered as the waves passed under them.

When we set off it was a brilliant morning of April, and the green, glittering waves seemed to toss the canoe among themselves, yet as we drew nearer this island a sudden thunderstorm broke out behind the rocks we were approaching, and lent a momentary tumult to this still vein of the Atlantic.

We landed at a small pier, from which a rude track leads up to the village between small fields and bare sheets of rock like those in Aranmor. The youngest son of my boatman, a boy of about seventeen, who is to be my teacher and guide, was waiting for me at the pier, and guided me to his house, while the men settled the curagh and followed slowly with my baggage.

My room is at one end of the cottage, with a boarded floor and ceiling, and two windows opposite each other. Then there is the kitchen with earth floor and open rafters, and two doors, opposite each other, opening into the open air, but no windows. Beyond it there are two small rooms of half the width of the kitchen with one window apiece.

The kitchen itself, where I will spend most of my time, is full of beauty and distinction. The red dresses of the women who cluster round the fire on their stools give a glow of almost Eastern richness, and the walls have been toned by the turf-smoke to a soft brown that blends with the grey earth-colour of the floor. Many sorts of fishing-tackle, and the nets and oil-skins of the men, are hung upon the walls or among the open rafters; and right overhead under the thatch, there is a whole cowskin from which they make pampooties.*

Every article on these islands has an almost personal character, which gives this simple life, where all art is unknown, something of the artistic beauty of medieval life. The curaghs and spinning-wheels, the tiny wooden barrels that are still much used in the

---

* Pampooties are rawhide shoes worn on the Aran Islands, and one of the few remaining items of folk dress. Once used widely all over Ireland.

place of earthenware, the home-made cradles, churns and baskets, are all full of individuality, and being made from materials that are common here, yet to some extent peculiar to the island, they seem to exist as a natural link between the people and the world that is about them.

The simplicity and unity of the dress increases in another way the local air of beauty. The women wear red petticoats and jackets of the island wool stained with madder, to which they usually add a plaid shawl twisted round their chests and tied at their backs. When it rains they throw another petticoat over their heads with the waistband round their faces or, if they are young, they use a heavy shawl like those worn in Galway. Occasionally other wraps are worn, and during the thunderstorm I arrived in I saw several girls with men's waistcoats buttoned round their bodies. Their skirts do not come much below the knee, and show their powerful legs in the heavy indigo stockings with which they are all provided.

The men wear three colours: the natural wool, indigo, and a grey flannel that is woven of alternate threads of indigo and the natural wool. In Aranmor many of the younger men have adopted the usual fisherman's jersey, but I have only seen one on this island.

As flannel is cheap – the women spin the yarn from the wool of their own sheep and it is then woven by a weaver in Kilronan for fourpence a yard—the men seem to wear an indefinite number of waistcoats and woollen drawers one over the other. They are usually surprised at the lightness of my own dress, and one old man I spoke to for a minute on the pier, when I came ashore, asked me if I was not cold with 'my little clothes'.

As I sat in the kitchen to dry the spray from my coat, several men who had seen me walking up came in to talk to me, usually murmuring on the threshold 'The blessing of God on this place', or some similar words.

Michael (the boy who is teaching me Irish) walks so fast when I am out with him that I cannot pick my steps, and the sharp-edged fossils which abound in the limestone have cut my shoes to pieces.

The family held a consultation on them last night and in the end it was decided to make me a pair of pampooties, which I have been wearing today among the rocks.

They consist simply of a piece of raw cowskin, with the hair outside, laced over the toe and round the heel with two ends of fishing line that work round and are tied above the instep.

In the evening, when they are taken off, they are placed in a basin of water, as the rough hide cuts the foot and stocking if it is allowed to harden. For the same reason the people often step into the surf during the day, so that their feet are continually moist.

At first I threw my weight upon my heels, as one does naturally in a boot, and was a good deal bruised, but after a few hours I learned the natural walk of man, and could follow my guide in any portion of the island.

In one district below the cliffs, towards the north, one goes for nearly a mile jumping from one rock to another without a single ordinary step; and here I realized that toes have a natural use, for I found myself jumping towards any tiny crevice in the rock before me, and clinging with an eager grip in which all the muscles of my feet ached from their exertion.

While I am walking with Michael someone often comes to me to ask the time of day. Few of the people, however, are sufficiently used to modern time to understand in more than a vague way the convention of the hours, and when I tell them what o'clock it is by my watch, they are not satisfied, and ask how long is left them before the twilight.

The general ignorance of any precise hours in the day makes it impossible for the people to have regular meals. They seem to eat together in the evening, and sometimes in the morning, a little after dawn, before they scatter for their work, but during the day they simply drink a cup of tea and eat a piece of bread, or some potatoes, whenever they are hungry.

For men who live in the open air they eat strangely little. Often when Michael has been out weeding potatoes for eight or nine hours without food, he comes in and eats a few slices of home-made bread, and then he is ready to go out with me and wander for hours about the island.

They use no animal food except a little bacon and salt fish. The old woman says she would be very ill if she ate fresh meat. Some years ago, before tea, sugar and flour had come into general use, salt fish was much more the staple article of diet than at present, and, I am told, skin diseases were very common, though they are now rare on the islands.

No one who has not lived for weeks among these grey clouds and seas can realize the joy with which the eye rests on the red dresses of the women, especially when a number of them are to be found together, as happened early this morning.

I had heard that the young cattle were to be shipped for a fair on the mainland, which is to take place in a few days, and I went down on the pier, a little after dawn, to watch them.

The bay was shrouded in the greys of coming rain, yet the thinness of the cloud threw a silvery light on the sea, and an unusual depth of blue to the mountains of Connemara.

As I was going across the sandhills one dun-sailed hooker glided slowly out to begin her voyage, and another beat up to the pier. Troops of red cattle, driven mostly by the women, were coming up from several directions, forming, with the green of the long tract of grass that separates the sea from the rocks, a new unity of colour.

The pier itself was crowded with bullocks and a great number of the people. I noticed one extraordinary girl in the throng who seemed to exert an authority on all who came near her. Her curiously formed nostrils and narrow chin gave her a witch-like expression, yet the beauty of her hair and skin made her singularly attractive.

When the empty hooker was made fast its deck was still many feet below the level of the pier, so the animals were slung down by a rope from the mast-head, with much struggling and confusion. Some of them made wild efforts to escape, nearly carrying their owners with them into the sea, but they were handled with wonderful dexterity, and there was no mishap.

When the open hold was filled with young cattle, packed as tightly as they could stand, the owners with their wives or sisters, who go with them to prevent extravagance in Galway, jumped down on the deck, and the voyage began. Immediately afterwards a rickety old hooker beat up with turf from Connemara and while she was unloading all the men sat along the edge of the pier and made remarks upon the rottenness of her timber till the owners grew wild with rage.

A week of sweeping fogs has passed over and given me a strange sensation of exile and desolation. I walk round the island nearly every day, yet I can see nothing anywhere but a mass of wet rock, a strip of surf and then a tumult of waves.

The slaty limestone has grown black with the water that is dripping on it, and wherever I turn there is the same grey obsession twining and wreathing itself among the narrow fields, and the same wail from the wind that shrieks and whistles in the loose rubble of the walls.

At first the people do not give much attention to the wilderness that is round them, but after a few days their voices sink in the kitchen, and their endless talk of pigs and cattle falls to the whisper of men who are telling stories in a haunted house.

It has cleared, and the sun is shining with a luminous warmth that makes the whole island glisten with the splendour of a gem, and fills the sea and sky with a radiance of blue light.

I have come out to lie on the rocks where I have the black edge of the north island in front of me, Galway Bay, too blue almost to look at, on my right, the Atlantic on my left, a perpendicular cliff under my ankles, and over me innumerable gulls that chase each other in a white cirrus of wings.

A nest of hooded crows is somewhere near me, and one of the old birds is trying to drive me away by letting itself fall like a stone every few minutes, from about forty yards above me to within reach of my hand.

Gannets are passing up and down above the Sound, swooping at times after a mackerel, and farther off I can see the whole fleet of hookers coming out from Kilronan for a night's fishing in the deep water to the west. As I lie here hour after hour I seem to enter into the wild pastimes of the cliff, and to become a companion of the cormorants and crows.

After Mass this morning an old woman was buried. She lived in the cottage next to mine, and more than once before noon I heard a faint echo of the keen.* I did not go to the wake for fear my presence might jar upon the mourners, but all last evening I could hear the strokes of a hammer in the yard where, in the middle of a little crowd of idlers, the next of kin laboured slowly at the coffin.

* Keen: Irish, *caoin*. A lament for the dead traditionally composed by special 'keening' women.

Today before the hour for the funeral, poteen* was served to a number of men who stood about upon the road and a portion was brought to me in my room. Then the coffin was carried out sewn loosely in sailcloth, and held near the ground by three cross-poles lashed upon the top. As we moved down to the low eastern portion of the island, nearly all the men, and all the oldest women, wearing petticoats over their heads, came out and joined in the procession.

While the grave was being opened the women sat down among the flat tombstones, bordered with a pale fringe of early bracken, and began the wild keen, or crying for the dead. Each old woman as she took her turn in the leading recitative, seemed possessed for the moment with a profound ecstasy of grief, swaying to and fro, and bending her forehead to the stone before her, while she called out to the dead with a perpetually recurring chant of sobs.

All round the graveyard other wrinkled women, looking out from under the deep red petticoats that cloaked them, rocked themselves with the same rhythm and intoned the inarticulate chant that is sustained by all as an accompaniment. The morning had been beautifully fine, but as they lowered the coffin into the grave, thunder rumbled overhead and hailstones hissed among the bracken.

In Inishmaan one is forced to believe in a sympathy between man and nature, and at this moment when the thunder sounded a death-peal of extraordinary grandeur above the voices of the women, I could see the faces near me stiff and drawn with emotion.

When the coffin was in the grave, and the thunder had rolled away, across the hills of Clare, the keen broke out again more passionately than before.

Old Pat Dirane (the storyteller) continues to come up every day to talk to me, and at times I turn the conversation to his experiences of the fairies.† He has seen a good many of them, he says, in different parts of the island, especially in the sandy districts

---

* Poteen: Irish, *poitin*. Illegally distilled whiskey.
† Fairies: in Irish, *Daoine Si* (People of the Shee) or 'Good Folk', traditionally supernatural and beautiful, they often stole away the living.

north of the slip. They are about a yard high with caps like the 'peelers'★ pulled down over their faces. On one occasion he saw them playing ball in the evening just above the slip, and he says I must avoid that place in the morning or after nightfall for fear they might do me mischief.

He has seen two women who were 'away' with them, one a young married woman, the other a girl. The woman was standing by a wall, at a spot he described to me with great care, looking out towards the north.

Another night he heard a voice crying out in Irish, '*Mhathair ta me marbh*' ('O mother, I'm killed'), and in the morning there was blood on the wall of his house, and a child in a house not far off was dead.

Yesterday he took me aside and said he would tell me a secret he had never yet told to any person in the world.

'Take a sharp needle,' he said, 'and stick it under the collar of your coat, and not one of them will be able to have power on you.'

Iron is a common talisman with barbarians, but in this case the idea of exquisite sharpness was probably present also, and perhaps some feeling for the sanctity of the instrument of toil, a folk belief that is common in Brittany.

The fairies are more numerous in Mayo than in any other county, though they are fond of certain districts in Galway, where the following story is said to have taken place:

'A farmer was in great distress as his crops had failed, and his cow had died on him. One night he told his wife to make him a fine new sack for flour before the next morning; and when it was finished he started off with it before the dawn.

'At that time there was a gentleman who had been taken by the fairies, and made an officer among them, and it was often people would see him, and he riding on a white horse at dawn and in the evening.

'The poor man went down to the place where they used to see the officer, and when he came by on his horse, he asked the loan of two hundred and a half of flour, for he was in great want.

'The officer called the fairies out of a hole in the rocks where they stored their wheat, and told them to give the poor man what

---

★ Peelers: policemen, so called after their founder, Sir Robert Peel.

he was asking. Then he told him to come back and pay him in a year, and rode away.

'When the poor man got home he wrote down the day on a piece of paper, and that day year he came back and paid the officer.'

When he had ended his story the old man told me that the fairies have a tenth of all the produce of the country, and make stores of it in the rocks.

BANSHEE

3

The Pug-Nosed Fox

SOMERVILLE & ROSS

The arduous post of Resident Magistrate in Ireland exists no more, but is forever immortalized in the story of Major Sinclair Yeates who left his regiment, and his home country, England, equipped with a feeling heart and the belief that two and two inevitably make four, whereas in Ireland they are just as likely to make five or three.

It was a blazing day in late August, following on forty-eight hours of blanketing sea-fog; a day for flannels and a languid game of croquet. Lady Jane, the grey mare lent to me by Flurry, had been demoralized by her summer at grass, and was in that peculiarly loathsome frame of mind that is a blend of laziness and bumptiousness. If I left her to her own devices she drowsed, stumbling, through the dust; if I corrected her, she pranced and pulled, and kicked up behind like a donkey. My huntsman, Doctor Jerome Hickey, who was to have been in the forefront of the photograph, was twenty miles off in an open boat, on his way to an island at the far end of his dispensary district, with fifteen cases of measles ahead of him. I envied him; measles or no, he had on a turned down collar. As a result of his absence I rode in solitary dignity at the head of the pack, or, to speak more correctly, I preceded Michael by some thirty yards of unoccupied road, while the pack, callous to flogging, and disdainful of my cajoleries, clave to the heels of Michael's horse.

In this order we arrived at the tryst, a heathery hillside, flanked by a dense and rambling wood. A seagull scream from the hillside announced the presence of my wife, and summoned me to join her and the photographer at the spot where they were encamped. I put the mare at a suitable place in the wall by the roadside. She refused it, which was not more than I had expected. I sampled my new spurs on her fat sides, with the result that she charged the wall, slantways, at the exact spot where Philippa had placed her bicycle against it, missed the bicycle by a hairsbreadth, landed in the field with a thump, on all four feet, and ended with two most distressing bucks. It was a consolation to me, when I came in touch again with the saddle, to find that one of the new spurs had ploughed a long furrow in her shoulder.

The photographer was a young man from Belfast, a newcomer to the neighbourhood; Philippa is also a photographer, a fact that did not tend as much as might have been expected to the harmony of the occasion.

'Mrs Yeates has selected this hillock,' said Mr McOstrich, in tones of acrid resignation, indicating as he spoke a sugar-loaf-shaped knoll, thickly matted with furze and heather. 'She considers the background characteristic. My own suggestion would have been the grass field yonder.'

It is an ancient contention of my wife that I, in common with all other men, in any dispute between a female relative and a tradesman, side with the tradesman, partly from fear, partly from masculine clannishness, and most of all from a desire to stand well with the tradesman. Nothing but the remembrance of this preposterous reproach kept me from accepting Mr McOstrich's point of view and, while I hesitated, Michael was already taking up his position on the hillock, perhaps in obedience to some signal from Philippa, perhaps because he had realized the excellent concealment afforded by the deep heather to his horse's fetlocks, whose outline was of a somewhat gouty type. It was part of Flurry Knox's demoniac gift for horseflesh that he should be able to buy screws and make them serve his exacting purposes. Michael's horse, Moses, had, at a distance, the appearance of standing upon four champagne bottles, but he none the less did the work of two sound horses and did it well.

I goaded Lady Jane through the furze, and established myself beside Michael on the sugar-loaf, the hounds disposed themselves in an interval of bracken below, and Mr McOstrich directed his camera upon us from an opposite slope.

'Show your teeth, please,' said Mr McOstrich to Michael. Michael already simmering with indignation at the senseless frivolity of the proceedings, glowered at his knuckles, evidently suspicious of an ill-timed pleasantry.

'Do you hear, Whip?' repeated Mr McOstrich, raising his bleak northern voice, 'show your teeth, please!'

'He only wants to focus us,' said I, foreseeing trouble, and hurriedly displaying my own new front row in a galvanic smile.

Michael murmured to Moses' withers something that sounded like a promise to hocus Mr McOstrich when occasion should serve, and I reflected on the hardship of having to feel apologetic towards both Michael and the photographer.

Only those who have participated in 'Hunt Groups' can realize the combined tediousness and tension of the moments that followed. To keep thirty hounds headed for the camera, to ensure that your horse has not closed its eyes and hung its head in a doze of boredom, to preserve for yourself that alert and workmanlike aspect that becomes a sportsman, and then, when these things have been achieved and maintained for what feels like a month, to see the tripod move in spider strides to a fresh position and know that all has to be begun over again. After several of these tentative selections of a site, the moment came when Mr McOstrich swung his black velvet pall in the air and buried his head under its portentous folds. The hounds, though uneasy, had hitherto been comparatively calm, but at this manifestation their nerve broke, and they unanimously charged the glaring monster in the black hood with loud and hysterical cries.

Had not Michael perceived their intention while there was time awful things might have happened. As it was, the leaders were flogged off with ignominy, and the ruffled artist returned from the rock to which he had fled. Michael and I arranged ourselves afresh upon the hillock; I squared my shoulders, and felt my wonted photographic expression of hang-dog desperation settle down upon me.

'The dogs are not in the picture, Whip!' said Mr McOstrich in the chill tone of outraged dignity.

I perceived that the hounds, much demoralized, had melted away from the slope in front of us, and were huddling in a wisp in the intervening hollow. Blandishments were of no avail; they wagged and beamed apologetically, but remained in the hollow. Michael, in whose sensitive bosom the term 'Whip' evidently rankled, became scarlet in the face and avalanched from the hilltop upon his flock with a fury that was instantly recognized by them. They broke in panic, and the astute and elderly Venus, followed by two of the young entry, bolted for the road. They were there met by Mr McOstrich's carman, who most creditably headed the puppies with yells and his driving-whip, but was outplayed by Venus, who, dodging like a football professional, doubled under the car horse, and fled irrevocably. Philippa, who had been flitting from rock to rock with her kodak, and unnerving me with injunctions as to the angle of my cap, here entered the lists with a packet of sandwiches, with which, in spite of the mustard, she restored a certain confidence to the agitated pack, a proceeding observed from afar with trembling indignation by Minx, her fox-terrier. By reckless expenditure of sandwich the hounds were tempted to their proper position below the horses, but, unfortunately, with their sterns to the camera, and their eyes fastened on Philippa.

'Retire, madam!' said Mr McOstrich, very severely, 'I will attract the dogs!'

Thus rebuked, Madam scrambled hastily over the crest of the hillock and sank in unseemly laughter into the deep heather behind it.

'Now, very quiet, please,' continued Mr McOstrich, and then unexpectedly uttered the words, 'Pop! Pop! Pop!' in a high soprano.

Michael clapped his hand over his mouth, the superseded siren in the heather behind me wallowed in fresh convulsions; the hounds remained unattracted.

Then arose, almost at the same moment, a voice from the wood behind us, the voice of yet a third siren, more potent than that of either of her predecessors, the voice of Venus hunting a line. For the space of a breath the hounds hung on the eager hacking yelps, in the next breath they were gone.

Matters now began to move on a serious scale, and with a speed that could not have been foreseen. The wood was but fifty yards from our sugar-loaf. Before Michael had got out his horn, the hounds were over the wall, before the last stern had disappeared the leaders had broken into full cry.

'Please God it might be a rabbit!' exclaimed Michael, putting spurs to his horse and bucketing down through the furze towards the wood, with blasts of the horn that were fraught with indignation and rebuke.

An instant later, from my point of vantage on the sugar-loaf, I saw a big and very yellow fox cross an open space of heather high up on the hill above the covert. He passed and vanished; in half a dozen seconds Venus, plunging through the heather, came shrieking across the open space and also vanished. Another all too brief an interval, and the remainder of the pack had stormed through the wood and were away in the open after Venus, and Michael, who had pulled up short on the hither side of the covert wall, had started up the hillside to catch them.

The characteristic background chosen by Philippa, however admirable in a photograph, afforded one of the most diabolical rides of my experience. Uphill, over courses of rock masked in furze bushes, round the head of a boggy lake, uphill again through deep and purple heather, over a horrid wall of long slabs half buried in it; past a ruined cabin, with thorn bushes crowding low over the only feasible place in the bank, and at last, the top of the hill, and Michael pulling up to take observations.

The best pack in the kingdom, schoolmastered by a regiment of whips, could not have precipitated themselves out of covert with more academic precision than had been shown by Flurry Knox's irregulars. They had already crossed the valley below us, and were running up a long hill as if under the conventional tablecloth; their cry, floating up to us, held all the immemorial romance of the chase.

Michael regarded me with a wild eye; he looked as hot as I felt, which was saying a good deal, and both horses were puffing.

'He's all the ways for Temple Braney!' he said. 'Sure I know him well—that's the pug-nosed fox that's in it these last three seasons, and it's what I wish ——'

(I regret that I cannot transcribe Michael's wish in its own terms, but I may baldly summarize it as a desire minutely and anatomically specified that the hounds were eating Mr McOstrich.)

Here the spurs were once more applied to Moses' reeking sides, and we started again, battering down the twists of a rocky lane into the steaming, stuffy valley. I felt as guilty and as responsible for the whole affair as Michael intended that I should feel; I knew that he even laid to my charge the disastrous appearance of the pug-nosed Temple Braney fox. (Whether this remarkable feature was a freak of nature, or of Michael's lurid fancy, I have never been able to ascertain.)

The valley was boggy, as well as hot, and the deep and sinuous ditch that by courtesy was supposed to drain it, was blind with rushes and tall fronds of *Osmunda regalis* fern. Where the landing was tolerable, the take-off was a swamp, where the take-off was sound the landing was feasible only for a frog; we lost five panting minutes, closely attended by horse-flies, before we somehow floundered across and began the ascent of the second hill. To face tall banks, uphill, is at no time agreeable, especially when they are enveloped in a jungle of briars, bracken, and waving grass, but a merciful dispensation of cow-gaps revealed itself; it was one of the few streaks of luck in a day not conspicuous for such.

At the top of the hill we took another pull. This afforded to us a fine view of the Atlantic, also of the surrounding county and all that was therein with, however, the single unfortunate exception of the hounds. There was nothing to be heard save the summery rattle of a reaping-machine, the strong and steady rasp of a corn-crake, and the growl of a big steamer from a band of fog that was advancing, ghost-like, along the blue floor of the sea. Two fields away a man in a straw hat was slowly combing down the flanks of a haycock with a wooden rake, while a black and white cur slept in the young after-grass beside him. We broke into their sylvan tranquillity with a heated demand whether the hounds had passed that way. Shrill clamour from the dog was at first the only reply; its owner took off his hat, wiped his forehead with his sleeve, and stared at us.

'I'm as deaf as a beetle this three weeks,' he said, continuing to look us up and down in a way that made me realize, if possible, more than before, the absurdity of looking like a Christmas card in the heat of a summer's day.

'Did ye see the *Hounds*?' shouted Michael, shoving the chestnut up beside him.

'It's the neurology I got,' continued the haymaker, 'an' the pain does be whistlin' out through me ear till I could mostly run into the say from it.'

'It's a pity ye wouldn't,' said Michael, whirling Moses round, 'an' stop in it! Whisht! Look over, sir! Look over!'

He pointed with his whip along the green slopes. I saw, about half a mile away, two boys standing on a fence, and beyond them some cattle galloping in a field: three or four miles farther on the woods of Temple Braney were a purple smear in the hazy heat of the landscape. My heart sank; it was obvious even to my limited capacities that the pug-nosed fox was making good his line with a straightness not to be expected from one of his personal peculiarity, and that the hounds were still running as hard as ever on a scent as steamingly hot as the weather. I wildly thought of removing my coat and leaving it in charge of the man with neuralgia, but was restrained by the reflection that he might look upon it as a gift, flung to him in a burst of compassion, a misunderstanding that, in view of his affliction, it would be impossible to rectify.

I picked up my lathered reins and followed Michael at a gloomy trot in the direction of the galloping cattle. After a few fields a road presented itself, and was eagerly accepted by the grey mare, on whom the unbridled gluttonies of a summer's grass were beginning to tell.

'She's bet up, sir,' said Michael, dragging down a rickety gate with the handle of his whip. 'Folly on the road, there's a near way to the wood from the cross.'

Moses here walked cautiously over the prostrate gate.

'I'm afraid you'll kill Moses,' said I, by no means pleased at the prospect of being separated from my Intelligence Department.

'Is it him?' replied Michael, scanning the country ahead of him with hawk eyes. 'Shure he's as hardy as a throut!'

The last I saw of the trout was his bottle fetlocks disappearing nimbly in bracken as he dropped down the far side of a bank.

I 'follied on the road' for two stifling miles. The heavy air was pent between high hedges hung with wisps of hay from passing carts (hay-carrying in the south-west of Ireland conforms to the leisure of the farmer rather than to the accident of season); phalanxes of flies arose as if at the approach of royalty, and accompanied my progress at a hunting jog, which, as interpreted by Lady Jane, was an effective blend of a Turkish bath and a churn.

The 'near way' from the crossroads opened seductively with a lane leading to a farmhouse, and presently degenerated into an unfenced but plausible cart track through the fields. Breaches had been made in the banks for its accommodation, and I advanced successfully towards the long woods of Temple Braney, endeavouring, less successfully, to repel the attentions of two young horses, who galloped, squealed, and bucked round me and Lady Jane with the imbecile pleasantry of their kind. The moment when

I at length slammed in their faces the gate of the wood was one of sorely needed solace.

Then came the sudden bath of coolness and shade, and the gradual realization that I did not in the least know what to do next. The air was full of the deeply preoccupied hum of insects, and the interminable monologue of a wood pigeon; I felt as if I ought to apologize for my intrusion. None the less I pursued a ride that crossed the wood, making persevering efforts to blow my horn, and producing nothing but gramophonic whispers, fragmentary groans, and a headache. I was near the farther side of the wood when I saw fresh hoof-tracks on a path that joined the ride; they preceded me to a singularly untempting bank, with a branch hanging over it, and a potato-field beyond it. A clod had been newly kicked out of the top of it; I could not evade the conviction that Michael had gone that way. The grey mare knew it too, and bundled on to and over the bank with surprising celerity, and dropped skilfully just short of where the potato beds began. An old woman was digging at the other side of the field, and I steered for her, making a long tack down a deep furrow between the 'lazy-beds'.

'Did you see the hounds, ma'am?' I called out across the intervening jungle of potato stalks.

'Sir!'

She at all events was not deaf. I amended my inquiry.

'Did you see any dogs, or a man in a red coat?'

'Musha, bad cess to them, then I did!' bawled the old woman, 'look at the thrack o' their legs down thro' me little pratie garden! 'Twasn't but a whileen ago that they come leppin' out o' the wood to me, and didn't I think 'twas the Divil and all his young ones, an' I thurn meself down in the thrinch the way they wouldn't see me, the Lord save us!'

My heart warmed to her; I also would gladly have lain down among the umbrageous stalks of the potatoes, and concealed myself for ever from Michael and the hounds.

'What way did they go?' I asked, regretfully dismissing the vision, and feeling in my pocket for a shilling.

'They went wesht the road, your Honour, an' they screeching always; they crossed out the field below over-right the white pony, and faith ye couldn't hardly see Michael Leary for the shweat! God help ye asthore, yourself is getting hardship from them as well as another!'

The shilling here sank into her earthy palm, on which she prayed passionately that the saints might be surprised at my success. I felt that as far as I was concerned the surprise would be mutual; I had had nothing but misfortune since ten o'clock that morning, and there seemed no reason to believe that the tide had turned.

The pony proved to be a white mule, a spectral creature, standing in malign meditation trace-high in bracken; I proceeded in its direction at a trot, through clumps of bracken and coarse grass, and as I drew near, it uttered a strangled and heart-broken cry of greeting. At the same moment Lady Jane fell headlong on to her nose and the point of her right shoulder. It is almost superfluous to observe that I did the same thing. As I rolled on my face in the bracken, something like a snake uncoiled itself beneath me and became taut; I clutched at it, believing it to be the reins, and found I was being hung up, like clothes on a line, upon the mule's tethering rope. Lady Jane had got it well round her legs, and had already fallen twice in her efforts to get up, while the mule, round whose neck the tether rope had been knotted, was backing hard, like a dog trying to pull its head through its collar.

In sunstroke heat I got out my knife, and having cut the rope in two places, an operation accomplished in the depths of a swarm of flies and midges, I pulled the mare on to her legs. She was lame on the off fore, and the rope had skinned her shins in several places; my own shoulder and arm were bruised, and I had broken a stirrup leather. Philippa and the photographer had certainly provided me with a day of varied entertainment, and I could not be sure that I had even yet drained the cup of pleasure to the dregs.

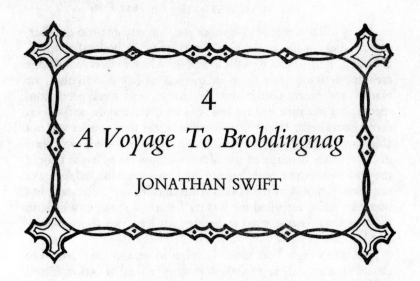

4

A Voyage To Brobdingnag

JONATHAN SWIFT

During this storm, which was followed by a strong wind west-south-west, we were carried by my computation about five hundred leagues to the east, so that the oldest sailor aboard could not tell in what part of the world we were. Our provisions held out well, our ship was staunch, and our crew all in good health; but we lay in the utmost distress for water. We thought it best to hold on the same course, rather than turn more northerly, which might have brought us to the north-west parts of Great Tartary, and into the Frozen Sea.

On the 16th day of June, 1703, a boy on the top-mast discovered land. On the 17th, we came in full view of a great island or continent (for we knew not whether) on the south side whereof was a small neck of land jutting out into the sea, and a creek too shallow to hold a ship of above one hundred tons. We cast anchor within a league of this creek, and our captain sent a dozen of his men, well armed, in the long boat, with vessels for water, if any could be found. I desired his leave to go with them, that I might see the country, and make what discoveries I could.

When we came to land, we saw no river or spring, nor any sign of inhabitants. Our men therefore wandered on the shore, to find out some fresh water near the sea, and I walked alone about a mile on the other side, where I observed the country all barren and rocky. I now began to be weary and, seeing nothing to entertain my curiosity, I returned gently down towards the creek; and the sea being full in my view, I saw our men already got into the boat, and rowing for life to the ship. I was going to hollo after them, although it had been to little purpose, when I observed a huge creature walking after them in the sea, as fast as he could; he waded not much deeper than his knees, and took prodigious strides; but our men had the start of him half a league, and the sea thereabouts being full of sharp-pointed rocks the monster was not able to overtake the boat. This I was afterwards told, for I durst not stay to see the issue of the adventure, but ran as fast as I could the way I first went, and then climbed up a steep hill, which gave me some prospect of the country. I found it fully cultivated; but that which first surprised me was the length of the grass which, in these grounds that seemed to be kept for hay, was about twenty feet high.

I fell into a high road, for so I took it to be, though it served to the inhabitants only as a footpath through a field of barley. Here I walked on for some time, but could see little on either side, it being now at least harvest, and the corn rising near forty feet.

I was an hour walking to the end of this field, which was fenced in with a hedge of at least one hundred and twenty feet high, and the trees so lofty that I could make no computation of their altitude. There was a stile to pass from this field into the next. It had four steps, and a stone to cross over when you came to the uppermost. It was impossible for me to climb this stile, because every step was six feet high, and the upper stone above twenty.

I was endeavouring to find some gap in the hedge, when I discovered one of the inhabitants in the next field, advancing towards the stile, of the same size with him I saw in the sea, pursuing our boat. He appeared as tall as an ordinary spire-steeple and took about ten yards at every stride, as near as I could guess. I was struck with the utmost fear and astonishment, and ran to hide myself in the corn, from whence I saw him at the top of the stile, looking back into the next field on the right hand, and heard him call in a voice many degrees louder than a speaking trumpet; but the noise was so high in the air that at first I certainly thought it was thunder.

Whereupon, seven monsters like himself came towards him with reaping-hooks in their hands, each hook about the largeness of six scythes. These people were not so well clad as the first, whose servants or labourers they seemed to be; for upon some words he spoke, they went to reap the corn in the field where I lay.

I kept from them at as great a distance as I could, but was forced to move with extreme difficulty, for the stalks of the corn were sometimes not above a foot distant, so that I could hardly squeeze my body betwixt them.

However, I made shift to go forward, till I came to a part of the field where the corn had been laid by the rain and wind. Here it was impossible for me to advance a step; for the stalks were so interwoven that I could not creep through, and the beards of the fallen ears so strong and pointed that they pierced through my clothes into my flesh. At the same time I heard the reapers not above a hundred yards behind me. Being quite dispirited with toil, and wholly overcome by grief and despair, I lay down between two ridges, and heartily wished I might there end my days. I bemoaned my desolate widow and fatherless children. I lamented my own folly and wilfulness in attempting a second voyage against the advice of all my friends and relations.

In this terrible agitation of mind I could not forbear thinking of Lilliput, whose inhabitants looked upon me as the greatest prodigy that ever appeared in the world: where I was able to draw an imperial fleet in my hand, and perform those other actions, which will be recorded for ever in the chronicles of that empire, while posterity shall hardly believe them, although attested by millions. I reflected what a mortification it must prove to me to appear as inconsiderable in this nation as one single Lilliputian would be among us. But this I conceived, was to be the least of my misfortunes; for, as human creatures are observed to be more savage and cruel in proportion to their bulk, what could I expect but to be a morsel in the mouth of the first among these enormous barbarians that should happen to seize me?

Undoubtedly philosophers are in the right when they tell us that nothing is great or little otherwise than by comparison. It might have pleased fortune to let the Lilliputians find some nation where the people were as diminutive with respect to them as they were to me. And who knows but that even this prodigious race of mortals might be equally overmatched in some distant part of the world whereof we have yet no discovery?

Scared and confounded as I was, I could not forbear going on with these reflections, when one of the reapers, approaching within ten yards of the ridge where I lay, made me apprehend that with the next step I should be squashed to death under his foot, or cut in two with his reaping-hook. And therefore, when he was again about to move, I screamed as loud as fear could make me. Where-upon the huge creature trod short, and looking round about under him for some time, at last espied me as I lay on the ground.

He considered awhile, with the caution of one who endeavours to lay hold on a small dangerous animal, in such a manner that it may not be able either to scratch or to bite him, as I myself have sometimes done with a weasel.

At length he ventured to take me up behind by the middle, between his forefinger and thumb, and brought me within three yards of his eyes, that he might behold my shape more perfectly. I guessed his meaning, and my good fortune gave me so much presence of mind that I resolved not to struggle in the least, as he held me in the air, about sixty feet from the ground, although he grievously pinched my sides, for fear I should slip through his fingers. All I ventured was to raise my eyes towards the sun, and place my hands together in a supplicating posture, and to speak some words in a humble, melancholy tone, suitable to the condition I then was in. For I apprehended every moment that he would dash me against the ground, as we usually do any little, hateful animal which we have a mind to destroy. But my good star would have it that he appeared pleased with my voice and gestures, and began to look upon me as a curiosity, much wondering to hear me pronounce articulate words, although he could not understand them.

In the meantime I was not able to forbear groaning and shedding tears, and turning my head towards my sides, letting him know, as well as I could, how cruelly I was hurt by the pressure of his thumb and finger. He seemed to apprehend my meaning; for, lifting up the lappet of his coat, he put me gently into it, and immediately ran along with me to his master, who was a substantial farmer, and the same person I had first seen in the field.

The farmer having (as I supposed by their talk) received such an account of me as his servant could give him, took a piece of a small straw, about the size of a walking-staff, and therewith lifted up the lappets of my coat, which, it seems, he thought to be some kind of covering that Nature had given me. He blew my hairs aside, to take a better view of my face. He called his hinds about him and asked them (as I afterwards learned) whether they had ever seen in the fields any little creature that resembled me: he then placed me softly on the ground upon all fours, but I got immediately up, and walked slowly backwards and forwards to let these people see I had no intent to run away.

They all sat down in a circle about me, the better to observe my motions. I pulled off my hat, and made a low bow towards the farmer. I fell on my knees, and lifted up my hands and eyes, and spoke several words as loud as I could: I took a purse of gold out of my pocket, and humbly presented it to him. He received it on the palm of his hand, then applied it close to his eye, to see what it was and afterwards turned it several times with the point of a pin (which he took out of his sleeve) but could make nothing of it. Whereupon I made a sign that he should place his hand on the ground.

I then took the purse and opening it, poured all the gold into his palm. There were six Spanish pieces, of four pistoles each, besides twenty or thirty smaller coins. I saw him wet the tip of his little finger upon his tongue, and take up one of my largest pieces, and then another, but he seemed to be wholly ignorant what they were. He made me a sign to put them again into my purse, and the purse again into my pocket, which, after offering it to him several times, I thought it best to do.

The farmer by this time was convinced I must be a rational creature. He spoke often to me, but the sound of his voice pierced my ears like that of a water-mill, yet his words were articulate enough. I answered as loud as I could in several languages, and he often laid his ear within two yards of me; but all in vain, for we were wholly unintelligible to each other. He then sent his servants to their work, and, taking his handkerchief out of his pocket, he doubled and spread it on his left hand, which he placed flat on the ground, with the palm upwards, making me a sign to step into it, as I could easily do, for it was not above a foot in thickness. I thought it my part to obey, and, for fear of falling, laid myself at length upon the handkerchief, with the remainder of which he lapped me up to the head for further security, and in this manner carried me home to his house. There he called his wife and showed me to her; but she screamed and ran back, as women do at the sight of a toad or a spider. However, when she had a while seen my behaviour, and how well I observed the signs her husband made, she was soon reconciled, and by degrees, grew extremely tender of me.

It was about twelve at noon, and a servant brought in dinner. It was only one substantial dish of meat (fit for the plain condition

of an husbandman), in a dish of about four and twenty feet dia-
meter. The company were the farmer and his wife, three children,
and an old grandmother. When they were set down, the farmer
placed me at some distance from him on the table, which was
thirty feet high from the floor. I was in a terrible fright, and kept
as far as I could from the edge, for fear of falling. The wife minced
a bit of meat, then crumbled some bread on a trencher, and
placed it before me. I made her a low bow, took out my knife and
fork and fell to eat, which gave them exceeding delight. The
mistress sent her maid for a small dram cup, which held about two
gallons and filled it with drink. I took up the vessel with much
difficulty in both hands, and in a most respectful manner, drank
to her ladyship's health, expressing the words as loud as I could in
English, which made the company laugh so heartily that I was
almost deafened with the noise. This liquor tasted like a small cider
and was not unpleasant.

Then the master made me a sign to come to his trencher-side,
but as I walked on the table, being in great surprise all the time, as
the indulgent reader will easily conceive and excuse, I happened to
stumble against a crust, and fell flat on my face, but received no
hurt. I got up immediately, and observing the good people to be
in much concern, I took my hat (which I held under my arm out
of good manners) and, waving it over my head, made three
huzzas, to show I had got no mischief by my fall.

But advancing forward towards my master (as I shall henceforth
call him), his youngest son, who sat next him, an arch boy of
about ten years old, took me up by the legs and held me so high
in the air that I trembled every limb; but his father snatched me
from him, and at the same time gave him such a box on the left ear
as would have felled an European troop of horses to the earth,
ordering him to be taken from the table. But being afraid the boy
might owe me a spite, and well remembering how mischievous all
children among us naturally are to sparrows, rabbits, young kittens
and puppy dogs, I fell on my knees and, pointing to the boy, made
my master to understand as well as I could that I desired his son
might be pardoned. The father complied and the lad took his
seat again; whereupon I went up to him and kissed his hand which
my master took and made him stroke me gently with it.

In the midst of dinner, my mistress's favourite cat leaped into
her lap. I heard a noise behind me like that of a dozen stocking-
weavers at work and turning my head I found it proceeded from

the purring of that animal, who seemed to be three times larger than an ox as I computed by the view of her head and one of her paws, while her mistress was feeding and stroking her. The fierceness of this creature's countenance altogether discomposed me, though I stood at the farther end of the table above fifty feet off, and although my mistress held her fast for fear she might give a spring and seize me in her talons.

But it happened there was no danger, for the cat took not the least notice of me when my master placed me within three yards of her. And as I have been always told and found true by experience in my travels that flying or discovering fear before a fierce animal is a certain way to make it pursue or attack you, so I resolved in this dangerous juncture to show no manner of concern. I walked with intrepidity five or six times before the very head of the cat and came within half a yard of her, whereupon she drew herself back as if she were more afraid of me. I had less apprehension concerning the dogs, whereof three or four came into the room as it is usual in farmers' houses, one of which was a mastiff equal in bulk to four elephants, and a greyhound somewhat taller than the mastiff, but not so large.

When dinner was almost done, the nurse came in with a child of a year old in her arms who immediately spied me and began a squall that you might have heard from London Bridge to Chelsea, after the usual oratory of infants to get me for a plaything. The mother out of pure indulgence took me up and put me towards the child, who presently seized me by the middle and got my head into his mouth where I roared so loud that the urchin was frightened and let me drop and I should infallibly have broke my neck if the mother had not held her apron under me. The nurse, to quiet the babe, made use of a rattle which was a kind of hollow vessel filled with great stones, and fastened by a cable to the child's waist; but all in vain, so that she was forced to apply the last remedy by nursing it.

When dinner was done my master went out to his labourers, and, as I could discover by his voice and gesture, gave his wife a strict charge to take care of me. I was very much tired and disposed to sleep, which my mistress perceiving, she put me on her own bed and covered me with a clean white handkerchief, but larger and coarser than the mainsail of a man-of-war.

5

Elegy On The Death Of A Mad Dog

OLIVER
GOLDSMITH

Good people all, of every sort,
  Give ear unto my song;
And if you find it wondrous short —
  It cannot hold you long.

In Islington there was a man,
  Of whom the world might say,
That still a godly race he ran —
  Whene'er he went to pray.

A kind and gentle heart he had,
  To comfort friends and foes;
The naked every day he clad —
  When he put on his clothes.

And in that town a dog was found,
  As many dogs there be,
Both mongrel, puppy, whelp, and hound,
  And curs of low degree.

This dog and man at first were friends;
  But when a pique began,
The dog, to gain some private ends,
  Went mad and bit the man.

Around from all the neighbouring streets
  The wondering neighbours ran,
And swore the dog had lost his wits,
  To bite so good a man.

The wound it seemed both sore and sad
  To every Christian eye;
And while they swore the dog was mad,
  They swore the man would die.

But soon a wonder came to light,
  That showed the rogues they lied:
The man recovered from the bite,
  The dog it was that died.

6

In The Wood Of Coilla Doraca

JAMES STEPHENS

The opening chapter, 'The Coming of Pan', in the marvellous adventures of the children, Seamus Beg, Brigid Beg, the Thin Woman of Inis Magrath, and the Leprechauns of Gort na Cloca Mora:

In the centre of the pine wood called Coilla Doraca there lived not long ago two Philosophers. They were wiser than anything else in the world except the Salmon who lies in the pool of Glyn Cagny into which the nuts of knowledge fall from the hazel bush on its bank. He, of course, is the most profound of living creatures, but the two Philosophers are next to him in wisdom. Their faces looked as though they were made of parchment, there was ink under their nails, and every difficulty that was submitted to them, even by women, they were able to instantly resolve. The Grey Woman of Dun Gortin and the Thin Woman of Inis Magrath asked them the three questions which nobody had ever been able to answer, and they were able to answer them. That was how they obtained the enmity of these two women which is more valuable than the friendship of angels. The Grey Woman and the Thin Woman were so incensed at being answered that they married the two Philosophers in order to be able to pinch them in bed, but the skins of the Philosophers were so thick that they did not know they were being pinched. They repaid the fury of the women with such tender affection that these vicious creatures almost expired of chagrin, and once, in a very ecstasy of exasperation, after having been kissed by their husbands, they uttered the fourteen hundred maledictions which comprised their wisdom, and these were learned by the Philosophers who thus became even wiser than before.

In due process of time two children were born of these marriages. They were born on the same day and in the same hour, and they were only different in this, that one of them was a boy and the other one was a girl. Nobody was able to tell how this had happened, and, for the first time in their lives, the Philosophers were forced to admire an event which they had been unable to prognosticate; but having proved by many different methods that the children were really children, that what must be must be, that a fact cannot be controverted, and that what has happened once may happen twice, they described the occurrence as extraordinary but not unnatural, and submitted peacefully to a Providence even wiser than they were.

The Philosopher who had the boy was very pleased because, he said, there were too many women in the world, and the Philosopher who had the girl was very pleased also because, he said, you cannot have too much of a good thing: the Grey Woman and the Thin Woman, however, were not in the least softened by maternity—they said that they had not bargained for it, that the children were gotten under false pretences, that they were respectable married women, and that, as a protest against their wrongs, they would not cook any more food for the Philosophers. This was pleasant news for their husbands, who disliked the women's cooking very much, but they did not say so, for the women would certainly have insisted on their rights to cook had they imagined their husbands disliked the results: therefore, the Philosophers besought their wives every day to cook one of their lovely dinners again, and this the women always refused to do.

They all lived together in a small house in the very centre of a dark pine wood. Into this place the sun never shone because the shade was too deep, and no wind ever came there either, because the boughs were too thick, so that it was the most solitary and quiet place in the world, and the Philosophers were able to hear each other thinking all day long, or making speeches to each other, and these were the pleasantest sounds they knew of. To them there were only two kinds of sounds anywhere—these were conversation and noise: they liked the first very much indeed, but they spoke of the second with stern disapproval, and, even when it was made by a bird, a breeze, or a shower of rain, they grew angry and demanded that it should be abolished. Their wives seldom spoke at all and yet they were never silent: they communicated with each other by a kind of physical telegraphy which they had learned among the Shee*—they cracked their finger-joints quickly or slowly and so were able to communicate with each other over immense distances, for by dint of long practice they could make great explosive sounds which were nearly like thunder, and gentler sounds like the tapping of grey ashes on a hearthstone. The Thin Woman hated her own child, but she loved the Grey Woman's baby, and the Grey Woman loved the Thin Woman's infant but could not abide her own. A compromise may put an end to the most perplexing of situations, and, consequently, the two women swapped children, and at once became the most tender and amiable mothers imaginable, and the families were able to live together in a more perfect amity than could be found anywhere else.

The children grew in grace and comeliness. At first the little boy was short and fat and the little girl was long and thin, then the little girl became round and chubby while the little boy grew lanky and wiry. This was because the little girl used to sit very quiet and be good and the little boy used not.

They lived for many years in the deep seclusion of the pine wood wherein a perpetual twilight reigned, and here they were wont to play their childish games, flitting among the shadowy trees like little quick shadows. At times their mothers, the Grey Woman and the Thin Woman, played with them, but this was seldom, and sometimes their fathers, the two Philosophers, came out and looked at them through spectacles which were very round and very glassy, and had immense circles of horn all round the edges. They had, however, other playmates with whom they could romp all day long. There were hundreds of rabbits running about in the brushwood; they were full of fun and were very fond of playing with the children. There were squirrels who joined cheerfully in their games, and some goats, having one day strayed in from the big world, were made so welcome that they always came again whenever they got the chance. There were birds also, crows and blackbirds and willy-wagtails, who were well acquainted with the youngsters, and visited them as frequently as their busy lives permitted.

* The fairy people.

At a short distance from their home there was a clearing in the wood about ten feet square; through this clearing, as through a funnel, the sun for a few hours in the summer time blazed down. It was the boy who first discovered the strange radiant shaft in the wood. One day he had been sent out to collect pine cones for the fire. As these were gathered daily the supply immediately near the house was scanty, therefore he had, while searching for more, wandered farther from his home than usual. The first sight of the extraordinary blaze astonished him. He had never seen anything like it before, and the steady, unwinking glare aroused his fear and curiosity equally. Curiosity will conquer fear even more than bravery will; indeed, it has led many people into dangers which mere physical courage would shudder away from, for hunger and love and curiosity are the great impelling forces of life. When the little boy found that the light did not move he drew closer to it, and at last, emboldened by curiosity, he stepped right into it and found that it was not a thing at all. The instant that he stepped into the light he found it was hot, and this so frightened him that he jumped out of it again and ran behind a tree. Then he jumped into it for a moment and out of it again, and for nearly half an hour he played a splendid game of tip and tig with the sunlight. At last he grew quite bold and stood in it and found that it did not burn him at all, but he did not like to remain in it, fearing that he might be cooked. When he went home with the pine cones he said nothing to the Grey Woman of Dun Gortin or to the Thin Woman of Inis Magarth or to the two Philosophers, but he told the little girl all about it when they went to bed, and every day afterwards they used to go and play with the sunlight, and the rabbits and the squirrels would follow them there and join in their games with twice the interest they had shown before.

7
Never No More

MAURA LAVERTY

I went to live with Gran* on October 4th, 1920. I cannot forget the date since it was also the date of my father's funeral.

It was settled that I should continue to attend the convent National School until the following summer twelvemonth, when Gran would send me to a boarding school. When I came from school every day Bran, our toothless sheepdog, met me at the foot of the long boreen that we insisted on miscalling 'avenue'. His rheumaticky caperings accompanied me between the rime-touched hedges where fat scarlet haws and orange Johnny M'Goreys glowed defiance to the frost.

Derrymore House was a comfortable two-storeyed building with a slated roof. The ground floor was cut in two by a hall that ran from back door to front door. To the right were the parlour and the little bedroom where Mike Brophy slept. On the left was the big kitchen and, opening off it, the storeroom and the buttery. None of us ever entered the house by the hall-door. We always went around to the back where a big clamp of turf standing about twenty feet from the house shut off from the kitchen windows the haggard with its cow-house, pig-stye and hen-run.

On cold days it was good to reach the bright comfort of Grandmother's kitchen where the big fireplace that could hold a kish of turf sent out a scorching heat.

Judy Ryan, Grandmother's servant-girl, always had my dinner

* In Ballyderrig, on the edge of the great bog of Allen.

ready for me on the white-scrubbed table that stood against the
wall in the space between the two big windows with their ribbon-
looped lace curtains and pots of geraniums. Sometimes Mike
Brophy, the labouring man, would be sitting at the fire having a
shin-heat before going out to milk the cows. More often than not,
Heck Murray would be there, too, hugging himself with his short
arms and giggling now and again at some private joke of his own.
Poor Heck was a simpleton who practically lived at Gran's house,
where he got his meals, an odd few shillings and a corner of his
own beside the fire.

Judy and myself enjoyed Heck. A red-headed little block of a
creature with a toothless grin and poor unsteady eyes, he might
have been any age from forty to sixty. When he wanted to
wheedle anything out of Gran, he always referred to himself as
'a poor orphint'. 'Sure, you wouldn't turn the back of your hand
to me, Mrs Lacy?' he would whimper. 'I'm only a poor orphint
wid me father and mother lyin' under the sod.' He was always
talking about a great match that was arranged for him with a girl
in Robertstown, and from time to time he had invited everyone in
Ballyderrig to the wedding. Judy and myself used to tease him
about the Big Night that never came off, but he always made out
that we were jealous. He had a grand way of half-remembering
riddles and of throwing them out at us, running question and
answer together inextricably.

'Ha! this'll tie yez into a knot!' he would gloat. 'Undher the-
wather - and - over - the - wather - an - egg - in - a - duck's - backside
—what's that?' Naturally, we were without an answer, whereupon Heck would rock with triumph. 'Ha! Heck's too smart for
yez! Heck has yez puzzled!'

While I ate my dinner, Gran sat beside me with her knitting,
questioning me on the day's events. She had an insatiable curiosity,
and I'm afraid I often made up gossip concerning the doings at
school just to please her.

When I had finished and the dishes were washed and placed
on the dresser, Grandmother beckoned me into the buttery to
help her with her baking. It was then I entered Heaven, for my
life held no keener pleasure than helping Grandmother to cook.
It was lovely to hustle around at her command, to watch that
busy spare little figure in its black dress and check apron and see
the brown loaves and currant cake and soda-bread take form under
her quick hands.

The buttery was a place of delight. It was lit by a small window placed high in the wall and covered with wire netting to prevent the entry of cats. Reaching half-way up its sides were bins for flour and oatmeal and flakemeal, and the yellow Indian meal for stir-about for fowl and humans. Above the bins was a stone ledge that held blue-rimmed crocks of cream and butter and eggs. And above these were wooden shelves for currants and raisins and sugar and spices. Directly under the window the ledge was left bare, for it was here that Gran did her cake-mixing.

Gran was different to most other women in Ballyderrig, in that she took a great interest in food. She was a splendid cook. Nothing new-fangled, mind you. None of your dressed-up dishes with fancy French names. But good honest Irish food cooked to perfection—ah! there Gran excelled. And if the savour and goodness of her cooking trapped you into eating more of it than was good for you, you could rely on her to make things right. Her head was a card-index file of amazing old herbal remedies. Many of them, I now suspect, were more amazing than remedial.

In my mind, Grandmother's cooking was inextricably mixed up with red-headed Johnny Doyle, the head of the tinker clan that descended on Ballyderrig at regular intervals, their carts piled high with children and tinware, and accompanied by herds of little shaggy black asses.

We found the tinkers decent people and honest to deal with, and Gran bought nearly all her cooking utensils from them. There was hardly one of her dishes that was not connected with Johnny Doyle's tinware, and as she cooked, her directions to those assisting her were punctuated with repetitions of the tinker's name.

'Grease me Johnny Doyle's big cake-tin,' she would say. 'I'm going to bake a treacle cake.' Or, 'Get out Johnny Doyle's pie-dish, Judy, till I set the beestings to curdle.' 'Take Johnny Doyle's little three-quart can with you,' she would tell me when I set out to gather mushrooms for the breakfast. And, on my return, 'Take one of Johnny Doyle's tin mugs and get yourself a drink of fresh buttermilk.'

Occasionally, the M'Canns, a rival tribe of tinkers, would drift into the town on the same day as the Doyles. At first, they would be friendly enough. But after two or three hours of steady drinking, they would begin to remember old feuds, and then the fun would commence, providing the people of Ballyderrig with the only excitement that ever came our way.

To describe the battle-scene, I shall have to describe Ballyderrig. The approach to the town is over a high canal bridge. The bridge slopes steeply down into a triangle out of which run Ballyderrig's two streets, with the village pump in the centre. The men of the village always ran to the top of the bridge to watch the fight in safety, for it wasn't wise to get in the way of the M'Canns and the Doyles when they were settling old scores and running up new ones.

Those were the days of the old R.I.C. [Royal Irish Constabulary]. The members of the British Constabulary were discreet men, and the sergeant and his three peelers always shut themselves into the barracks to play twenty-five until the tinkers had settled their differences.

No one took a greater interest in these fights than poor Rafferty, Paddy Lee's crazy son. A pale attenuated wraith of twenty-five, Rafferty would become wildly excited as he watched the fight from his vantage point on the bridge. Jumping with excitement, he would look down on the battle that raged around the pump. For some unexplained reason, his boots never possessed laces. In Ballyderrig, the laces which the men wore in their heavy hob-nailed boots were called 'fongs'. I was twenty before I knew the word should be 'thongs'.

Rafferty would shuffle up and down the bridge, his thin feet threatening at every step to leave behind them the heavy boots. Bursting with a desire to join in the fray, he would mutter over and over again:

'If I'd only a pair of fongs in me boots I'd bate the heads off the lot of them!'

I don't pretend to explain Rafferty. He was a phenomenon whose ways hinted at reincarnation, dual personality and other things beyond the ken of ordinary people. On moonlit nights in the midst of his ceaseless meanderings up and down the bridge, he would often stop suddenly and lift his pale, hollow-cheeked face to heaven. At such moments, the idiocy would leave his eyes which would blaze with a holy fire, and from the lips of this poor soft-brained creature would issue a flow of beautiful words in the accent of some place that was certainly not Ballyderrig. Where did he get these words? Not from the people among whom he lived. And the world of books was, of course, closed to him.

I remember watching him in fascination during one of those trances, frightened and thrilled by his words.

'A withered stick in a gap . . . a witch in a shivering rath,'

Rafferty was murmuring. And then he saw his father coming to take him home. All the fire left his face with its weak fuzz of fair beard. The old muddled look returned to his eyes and he broke into some jumbled nonsense about 'Freddie on the ice-cream'.

Rafferty was christened Patrick. I have often wondered if his nickname had anything to do with those poetic trances . . . if there lingered in the minds of those who dubbed him Rafferty some vague remembrances of Raftery, the blind poet.*

I always felt a great pity for Paddy Lee, the lad's father. He was a silent, heavy-footed man who went about the place with a stricken look on his white, grim face. His tender gentleness towards his idiot son was heartbreaking to see.

When Rafferty died I went to his wake. I hope I may never again hear such terrible sobs, dry and racking, as came from the man who would not be led from the little room where his son's corpse lay. And I am sure I shall never again see such beauty on a dead face as I saw on Rafferty's. To keep the flies from settling on his mouth and nostrils, his mother had covered his face with a veil such as children wear for their first Communion. Under the veil, the face might have been the death-mask of some great thinker . . . noble lofty brow, sensitive mouth, fine arched nose. And as I looked at him, ludicrously there leaped into my mind a picture of poor Rafferty hopping about on the bridge and begging for a pair of 'fongs' for his boots, so that he might beat the tinkers.

It was the women of the Doyles and M'Canns who fought out the battle to the bitter end. When the men of both sides had sustained a few cuts and bruises they always retired to one of our many public houses—eight of Ballyderrig's twelve shops sold liquor—to wash away their bitterness with porter. They lacked both the stamina and vindictiveness of the women. Great strapping women they were, with hair bleached like straw by the sun. Winter and summer, they wore their heavy mustard-coloured shawls. Enduring women, strong in fight and childbirth.

I often heard my father tell of how he passed a cartload of tinkers when on his way to Kildare one day. The cart was drawn up by the side of the road. A woman, obviously in labour, was being helped out of it and into a field.

* Raftery lived between 1784 and 1835, the last of the line of great Gaelic poets. He wandered the roads of Connacht, a poor blind fiddler.

Later in the day, when my father was returning from Kildare, he met the cart proceeding on its way. Sitting bolt upright in it, looking wan but at ease, was the mother. From the folds of her shawl came the wails of a new-born infant.

I'll never forget the day my grandmother delivered the tinker's baby.

Judy Ryan had just put the dinner on the table—pot-roasted rabbit, it was. Occasionally Mike Brophy would bring in three or four young rabbits . . . tender little coneens. Grandmother had a way of her own of coddling them in the baker with onions and slices of fat bacon and a little milk.

We were about to sit down to our meal when the cart clattered into the yard and came to a rest outside the kitchen window. A big bronzed giant of a fellow jumped from the cart and came to the door. He had the fear of death on his face.

Huddled on the floor of the cart was a woman who, at minute intervals, moaned hoarsely.

Grandmother sized up the situation at once.

'Bring her in,' she told the tinker briskly. With the help of Mike Brophy, the man got his wife out of the cart. She was a magnificently built woman. Her shirt-blouse of red plaid had slipped from her shoulders, disclosing the full rounded breasts that were white as haw blossom by contrast with her browned neck and face.

'Tch! tch!' said my grandmother, who was prudish about such things. 'Such a sight before the men!' She grabbed the woman's shawl from the cart and threw it hastily about her. Between them, the sobbing dark-eyed creature was half-carried up the stairs to the room over the kitchen.

'Get me plenty of hot water, Judy,' my grandmother called down. 'And tear up a couple of the old sheets for me.'

The tinkerman would not be coaxed from the foot of the stairs.

His frightened eyes, startlingly light blue in that dark face, looked at us from beneath the tousled fringe of black hair that came to his eyebrows.

'If I'd 'a known she was so near her time,' he said apologetically, 'we could 'a stayed in Edenderry. They'd 'a took her in at the Union.'

Suddenly, the gypsy seemed to reach the end of her endurance. Or maybe it was the relief of knowing herself in safe hands that brought about a reaction. In any case, she lost all self-control. Terrifying animal shrieks rent the house.

Mike Brophy, feeling that this was no place for a man, and obsessed by the average male's impulse to run away from suffering he cannot alleviate, sheepishly left the kitchen and wandered back to his work.

Between the shrieks I could hear my grandmother scolding the woman. She had little sympathy with complainers.

'You ought to be ashamed of yourself,' she was saying. 'A big strong woman like you to be carrying on like that. Stop it at once, I tell you, or out you'll go.'

This threat checked the tinker's hysteria and her shrieks ceased. Her husband continued to hang around the foot of the stairs, mumbling prayers and watching for my grandmother's appearance. Every now and then he'd shout up: 'How is she, ma'am? Is the babby all right?'

My grandmother afterwards told us that when she tried to comfort the suffering woman by commenting on this proof of her husband's solicitude, the tinker checked her moaning and smiled bitterly as she said:

'Aye, I know what's wrong wid him! Three months ago he gev me a batin' at the Fair of Athy. Ever since he's been out of his mind for fear it'd harm the babby.'

He had no need to worry. The baby arrived within an hour—a lovely black-eyed boy with plump sturdy limbs.

When the exhausted woman saw him, she stretched out a roughened but very gentle hand to fondle the little head that was covered with a surprisingly thick mat of silky black hair.

'Will you look at the head of hair on him?' she whispered proudly. ''Tis meself was nearly dead from that head of hair. Wasn't I kilt wid heartburn while I was carryin' him?'

From the sacred black trunk in her room that no one else was ever allowed to touch, Grandmother rooted out some of the little yellowed garments that had clothed her own babies, for the tinkers had come unprovided with as much as a shift for their firstborn. When the little one was dressed, I was allowed to sit and hold him.

Although Gran pretended to grumble at the extra work which the tinker's accouchement had brought on us, I could see she was in her element that evening. She hustled happily around, beating up eggs and milk with sugar and ginger for the beverage which we called 'smacks'. 'This'll put strength in the creature,' she said, pouring the smacks from one jug to another until it was a mass of sweet eggy froth.

To her horror, the tinkers wanted to move on that very evening. She looked at the man aghast.

'Is it mad you are?' she demanded. 'It would be the death of that woman to move her before the week is out.'

The tinker's eyes shifted before Grandmother's irate glance. 'I'm beholdin' to you for your kindness, ma'am,' he said. 'But, meanin' no offence, me mother never lay undher any of us for more'n a day.'

Reluctantly, he finally agreed to remain that night and the next. He refused to sleep in the house, saying that he'd feel smothered. 'If you'll take no exception,' he said, 'I'll sleep in the hayrick.' And so it was settled.

Not until the very last minute could he be brought to tear himself away from the baby that night. He sat there gloating over his son.

'Go on with you, man,' Grandmother said. 'You'd think there was never a baby born in the world before. With that fine woman you have upstairs, sure, you'll have a dozen more like him.'

On the third day, Grandmother saw that by no threats or coaxing could she keep the tinkers any longer. They were restless and ill at ease in this restricted world of walls and roofs and regular meals. They were eager for their own domain that was bounded only by the green hedges and the length of the long white road. Besides, they were anxious to join the rest of their clan at the Curragh Races.

Grandmother made them up a great basket of food.

'That woman of yours will be needing nourishment,' she said, putting in a dozen of brown eggs, a cartwheel of a currant cake, a fine piece of smoked bacon, and a roll of freshly made butter wrapped in muslin.

The broad-shouldered pair almost cried with gratitude as they said goodbye.

There were tears in my own eyes as they went, for I hated to see that sweet-smelling, sloe-eyed baby going out of my life. I watched them as they jolted down the boreen in their little cart drawn by the black ass that kicked its heels as if it, too, was glad to be facing once more the long days on the roads and the quiet nights under the stars.

When they reached the end of the boreen, the man turned and

waved his whip in farewell to the leggy little girl in her home-
made check frock. And the tinkerwoman lifted up the little
bundle in her arms so that I might have a last look at her son.

The tinkers still meet in Ballyderrig, but they tell me that the
fire has gone out of their fights and that the feud between the
Doyles and M'Canns is dying down. Well, the fights could not be
the same anyway—with poor Rafferty no longer there to shout
encouragement at them from the bridge.

8

Poet

PATRICK KAVANAGH

During the following winter and many winters after that, the fall of dark found me in my den up to my knees in scribbled paper. The corner of the room upstairs in which I worked was the North Pole of our house. It was often very cold.

'Come down before ye get yer death of cowld,' I would be advised.

I never heeded.

I used to sit on an old black chest opposite the table of an old sewing-machine on which a lighted candle dropped its grease. A hundred times at least I tried to write a poem on the candle but never got beyond the first line. On the walls of my room hung five holy pictures: 'The Virgin and Child,' 'Pope Leo XIII,' with his red robe and bald head, 'The Little Flower,' carrying a bouquet of roses or carnations, 'Saint Anthony of Padua,' wearing a wide halo, and last, but not least, our own 'Saint Patrick' prodding the snakes with the ferrule end of his crozier.

Down below in our kitchen visitors and customers were talking. Their conversation intruded a little at times on my mystic reveries. Johnnie of the Parables was there, relating the most profound metaphysics to the most homely parable. I thought Johnnie a bad construer of parables till now when I am trying to invent ones of my own to replace his which I have forgotten. He could tell a story to illustrate the working mechanism of an airplane engine or the movements of stardom.

'It's just like a wheel-plough on a rocky ridge,' he would begin, or: 'Ye might compare it to a man that was after comin' from America.' I never could see any comparative points. His other listeners would say: 'It's just like that, that's exactly how it is.'

Apart from his parables Johnnie was a pleasant talker and I should have been pleased to listen to him from any place other than the ivory tower.

Girls laughed in our kitchen and sometimes I caught enough of the joke to make me want to join the company.

The outside door rattled and a voice I recognized spoke. 'Paddy in?'

'He is, come on inside.'

'I wanted to get a heel on me boot. Where is he?'

'Patrick, Patrick, are ye comin' down? There's a man here wants a heel on his boot.'

I didn't answer.

'Are ye dead or alive?'

I rattled my boots on the floor to express irritation.

'Hello, hello, will ye throw a heel on this oul' boot? It'll not take ye five minutes.'

At that very moment the last line of a poem was dangling within my reach and now it was gone into the limbo of all unwritten things.

'Very well,' I said, 'I'll be down with you in a minute.'

'So that's what I was called for,' I said, examining the boot. 'That boot's first-class.'

'Listen,' he said. 'I've a great piece to tell you.'

I didn't want to hear. Like the little dog that destroyed Newton's life-work, this man didn't know the harm he had done. Six good lyrics are the price of immortality and perhaps one-sixth of immortality had been lost to me for the sake of an old boot.

'Troth, ye ought to stick to the trade,' Johnnie of the Parables said.

'That's what I do be tellin' him,' my mother added in support. Father was then going quite simple and took little interest in the talk.

About this time, too, a new farm was purchased for me; my mother's heart was in the land and her greatest wish was to see me set up as a strong farmer.

I bought an old bicycle and every week rode to Dundalk for the

Irish Statesman: sometimes I missed it and came home ready to fight or do anything nasty.

'As sour as a buck weasel,' was how my household described me on such occasions.

Once in the harvest time when I was working for a neighbour, I left the harvest field when we got the call to dinner. I rode to Dundalk in record time, got my paper and came back happy, though I had missed my dinner. One of the harvest men took the paper from my coat pocket where it lay among the sheaves. He turned the pages over.

'Begod,' he exclaimed, 'what the hell kind of a book is that?'

The roar of the reaper coming down the ledge blotted out my blasphemous reply.

As my name no more appeared in the Holy Poet's Corner, the neighbours concluded that I had given up the bardic game. The light in my window was a bit of a puzzle to many. Some said I was studying to be a policeman, which theory wasn't so far-fetched as you'd imagine: that very time a fellow called Crooked Paddy was being coached two nights a week by the local school-master for the examination to the Civic Guards. A few others thought I might be doing puzzles. My own household knew what I was up to, but they kept it close as it wasn't considered a respect-able occupation. My mother being a practical woman said to me time and again:

'I'm not against you writin' if I could see ye makin' anythin' of it.'

'You wait,' I told her. 'I'll be rich yet.'

'I don't see much signs of it now,' was all she could say.

'Christ,' I explained, 'sure I'm only at it a year or so. Shaw only made ten pounds before he was forty and now he's a millionaire.'

'Troth if ye'd mind yer little place it would fit ye better.'

'£ s. d.,' I cried, 'the only measuring-stick you peasants have is the one marked £ s. d.'

'The next thing is the people will be callin' ye "the bard",' one of my sisters said.

'Shakespeare was called the Bard of Avon.'

'You and yer Shakespeare.'

I sent a few poems to A. E.* and in about a week got a reply. He liked my verses, he said, and though he couldn't accept these,

* The poet, George William Russell, 1867–1935.

advised me to send him some more. A month later he accepted a poem from me; only the half of a poem in fact—the other half was written on a second page and got lost in the crowd.

I didn't see that poem in print till two years later. I missed that week's *Irish Statesman*. I got a pound for the poem, which came as a pleasant surprise. I never expected payment: I was quite innocent.

'Patrick, Patrick, the cows are after breakin' into the turnips,' I heard cried loudly.

I was sitting on my black box with a clean sheet on my knee. I felt that a magical poem was hovering near, ready to stray into my net of words.

'Aw, that's the lazy, lazy oul' divil.' Writing wasn't counted work. 'Will ye come down, I tell ye, before they destroy all the turnips?'

If it wasn't the turnips it was the pigs were after breaking loose, or a hen they wanted me help catch for the fowl dealer.

At nine o'clock the word came up to me:

'Come down, we're goin' to say the Rosary.' After waiting a few moments they sent me a second call: 'We're on our knees waitin' for ye to come down. If ye don't come down we'll start it without ye.'

'Well, start away,' I snapped.

'There can be neither luck nor grace in the house with ye, ye oul' Protestant ye. Go ahead, we'll say it without him.'

> '*Thou, O Lord, will open my lips*
> *And my tongue shall announce thy praise.*
> *Incline unto my aid, O God:*
> *O Lord, make haste to help me.*'

The beginning of the Rosary was very good poetry had habit not for me worn the keen edge off its surprise.

I came down and, kneeling beside a stool, threw my head on the stool and fell asleep. I am sure that should I ever have an attack of insomnia I need only have somebody start the Rosary and I'm cured. The Rosary in our house had been growing, growing steadily like a snowball, collecting prayers and pious ejaculations, till by the time of which I write it was a mile long. I mightn't complain too hard, for in other houses longitudinal additions to Rosaries had proceeded at a much greater speed. Litanies to this saint and that, prayers for intentions special and plain. I suggested on many occasions cutting the unwieldly end of our devotions, but my suggestion was vetoed as being grossly irreligious.

My brother Peter, who was now grown up, became my critic. Ablaze with the fire of creation I would come down and show him my latest poem. He read it quietly while I fidgeted about the floor waiting for the momentous decision.

'I think you have written better,' he said.

'For God's sake,' I cried, 'don't talk such nonsense. Read it again.'

'Read it for me,' mother said. 'I'd be able to give you a better opinion than you think.'

During this period father died. I wasn't really sorry, though my love for him had been very warm. His mind for two years before his death had been all mixed up. Names of people and things would dangle in his brain just beyond the rim of recollection. For instance, one day he thought of something that was associated with a spire or tower. I had become expert in this trouble of his: I ran up and down all the likely names and sounds connected with towers and churches. I used the word 'damn'—it occupied a prominent place in my vocabulary at any rate. Immediately father said 'I have it—campanile, a campanile tower.' When his mind was clear he compared his condition to Swift's. The Parish Priest—when I went to him to arrange for the burial service—said father was a lunatic. I told him he knew nothing about mental processes or psychology. The Parish Priest withdrew into the snail-box of dogma and refused to be drawn to discuss such a heterodox subject.

Father died in autumn. It is a fine thing to die when the leaves are falling and not when the cry of spring is among the hills. The earth that fell upon father's coffin covered in its fall one of the kindest, self-effacing, self-sacrificing of fathers and husbands. I remembered with joy the beatings he gave me. They had helped to make me pliant and resilient in a world where proud things get broken. I remembered the pally talks we had together, comparing lists of the stupidest men in the parish: my list corresponded with his in every name. Father told me how great was his wanderlust when he was young. He stayed at home to take care of his old mother. His care of his mother was one of the things for which he was famous in the district. I am not virtuous by my own good works. I am virtuous by nature. I have inherited my father's good works.

Peace to his soul.

Though no mortal woman has danced for me the angels of the sun have: upon the wavy skyline their silver slippers sparkled.

I was twenty-two years old.

Often on summer evenings when all the young people were dancing at some crossroads I wandered in petulant loneliness among the innocent of flower-land and tree-land. True, I sometimes was found among the mortal dancers in later years when I tried to have life both ways and had it neither. But in these rare moments of sweetness and light I remained true to myself, and poetry and vision were mine.

Old men and women colloguing in groups along the poplar-lined lane-way would suspend their conversation as I passed. Across the conversational breach they would hang a suspension bridge formed by the word 'and' 'Aaa ... nnn ... ddd.' Through the wide eyes of this bridge they would survey me with puzzled looks.

'And ... as I was sayin', she came up to me ... Is that Paddy Kavanagh? Would he be gettin' a bit odd of himself?'

Or some old farmer would stop to talk to me: 'The praties are doin' fine. 'Twill be a good year for the world. Yer not at the dance?' I was tempted to answer, yes, but I merely said: 'I didn't feel like it.'

'And yer far better off; this dancin' is all a cod. I never knew a good dancer was worth his grub to a farmer.'

From the tone of his speech I guessed that he thought me foolish in my wisdom.

I had just been writing a poem and it had come off, so I took a walk among the poplars as a thank-offering to the gods, but more because I had achieved something and was happy.

The gods of poetry are generous: they give every young poet a year's salary which he hasn't worked for; they let him take one peep into every tabernacle; they give him transcendent power at the start and ever after he must make his own magic. While he is learning the craft of verse and getting ready his tools they present him with wonderful lines which he thinks are his own.

In those days I had vision. I saw upon the little hills and in the eyes of small flowers beauty too delicately rare for carnal words.

'Do you see anything very beautiful and strange on those hills?' I asked my brother as we cycled together to a football match in Dundalk.

'This free-wheel is missing,' he said and he gave it a vigorous crack with the heel of his shoe.

'Is it on Drumgonnelly Hills?'

'Yes.'

'Do you mean the general beauty of the landscape?'

'Something beyond that, beyond that,' I said.

'Them hills are fine no doubt.'

'And is that all you see?'

'This free-wheel is missing again,' he said. 'I'll have to get down and put a drop of oil on it.'

We got moving again. 'What were we talking about?'

'Beauty,' I said.

And just then another football-follower caught up with us and the talk changed to such things as centre-forwards and half-backs and the prospects of the game. I was a football fan. Some of the pleasantest hours of my life were spent watching a game from the top of a wall near the Dundalk football ground. There were usually on this wall a dozen penniless followers of the game. We called it the Vincent de Paul grandstand.

Another day I mentioned this beauty to a bearded man: because he was bearded I thought him a mystic.

'Of course, of course ye can see things,' he said, 'sure any man that's a Catholic can see the Holy Ghost.'

I knew I had blundered, and I tried to change the subject, but the bearded one went on:

'When a man's confirmed, doesn't the Holy Ghost come down on him? Sure the bishops can talk to the Holy Ghost any time they like. And the priests too, if they want. Why, man, it's as simple as kiss yer hand.'

He said a lot more, till I swore that never again would I mention visions. Yet I did mention them.

Two men were leaning across the river bridge at Inniskeen. I think they were cattle-jobbers waiting for a train. Of their appearance I can only remember that they wore bowler hats and that one of them had a round patch on the upper of his boot. I was in the village for the morning newspaper. I stopped on the bridge and opened up a conversation with the two men. They were anxious to talk. A cattle-jobber out of a cattle-market is the silliest creature you could imagine, and this pair were no exception. They were weak on metaphysics.

We talked a long talk on religion which was relieved at intervals by some incongruous remarks on passing girls, the trout leaping in the stream below, and the price of cows.

'Can a Protestant get to Heaven?'

'Why not?' I said.

'And in that case one religion is as good as the next?'

'I heard a missioner to say,' the second jobber said, 'that he wasn't prepared to deny that there were some Protestants in Heaven.'

'That cow of Mullens' had a blind teat.'

I spoke of the beauty beyond beauty.

'I always said Inniskeen was as nice a spot as Rostrevor,' one of the jobbers claimed.

Towards the end of our talk the jobber in the bowler hat mentioned Shakespeare. I imagine he thought Shakespeare was at least a third cousin to God. As a schoolboy he had read *Othello*, he said. He read the play aloud to his father. His father wept and tore his hair, crying: 'Oh, if I could only get my hands on that scoundrel Iago!'

From that day forward I grew wise, but my innocent vision was gone. I had learned from Miss Cassidy's catechism that there was only one unforgivable sin—the sin against the Holy Ghost. Now I understood.

The Holy Ghost will not enter a soul that has not within it a secret room, free from vulgarity.

Yet though my candle of vision had been snuffed and the *Irish Statesman* no more, I still continued to write.

Having knocked and knocked and knocked at the door of Literature it was eventually opened, and then I did not want to enter. The clay of wet fields was about my feet and on my trouser-bottoms.

I was not a literary man. Poetry is not literature: poetry is the breath of young life and the cry of elemental beings: literature is a cold ghost-wind blowing through Death's dark chapel.

I turned from the door of Literature and continued my work among poetry, potatoes, and old boots.

9

The Mysterious Beggarman

BRÍD MAHON

The Fianna were a legendary band of heroes who once kept the peace of Ireland. Fionn was their leader. He had tested the salmon of knowledge and acquired second sight.

In Ireland there are four days in the year when the unseen world, which is all around us, draws near. These days are St Brigid's Eve, May Eve, St John's Eve and November Eve. People light bonfires on the hill-tops and if you make a wish at a certain moment in time between sunset and sunrise, it is sure to come true.

On this particular November Eve, a crimson sun hung low in the sky, turning the golden furze that covered Binn Eadair—The Hill of Howth—to bronze. The sea mist was lifting and a wind had blown up, shaking the trees of a great forest to the east where the wild boar fattened on acorns. Later, a town would be built across the ford of the hurdles where the river runs into the sea and that town would be called Dublin. But that was all in the future when Fionn and the Fianna would be no more than storybook names.

They had camped on the hill the night before and were now gathered down at the bay, a merry company of boys and young men with horses and dogs, eager for a day's hunting which would take them half-way across Ireland.

Fionn, the leader and captain, was in high good humour. He wet a finger and held it up. 'The wind is in the right direction.

As soon as Conan Maol finishes eating we'll sound the horns and be away.'

Conan was bald and fat and very greedy. He boasted he could eat five oxen on a weekday and as many more on Sunday.

'I'm still famished,' he grumbled and tore the last strip of meat from his bone. 'I should have gone to Tara with Caelte Mac Ronan. The king keeps a good table.'

'Even before you had reached the woods by the Black Pool, Caelte would have finished his journey,' a youth in green trews and a leather jerkin mocked.

Conan gave the boy a playful push, and then went to the water's edge to wash his face. He dipped the tail of his shirt in a pool and rubbed his bald head, his eyes and the tip of his nose. Then he shivered all over. He was woefully lazy and hated to wash.

He began to show off, skipping and sprinting and making little runs. 'I could easily overtake Caelte if I had a mind to,' he boasted. 'I can run faster than anyone.'

Behind him a quivering, crackling snore exploded in a mighty yawn and a sleepy voice declared: ''Tis an idle boast. I am the fastest thing on two feet.'

An old beggarman smothered in coats was rising out of a sand dune, and at the sight, Conan Maol let out a shout. 'Look at the champion. Forty coats and all and he thinks he can outrun me.'

The Fianna hooted with laughter and it was small wonder they did. The beggarman could hardly walk, let alone run and when he lifted a foot, the boot on the end of it squelched with the weight of mud that clung to the sole.

So distracted were they by the antics of the beggarman that they didn't notice a ship sail into the bay. The youth was the first to catch sight. He blinked, rubbed his eyes with his knuckles and blinked again. A tall, thin man was swinging himself out of the boat by means of a spear shaft. He was across the beach and on top of them before Conan Maol could say: 'By all the treasure in Tara, I swear this is a day for what you'd least expect. First, a boastful beggarman and now a roving, rusty seaman. Another champion I have no doubt.'

Conan was inclined to exaggerate, for to tell the truth the stranger was beautifully dressed in a cloak of scarlet caught up by a great golden brooch. He wore a silver helmet which came down so far that the only features visible were a sharp, pointed nose and an even sharper chin.

Fionn raised a hand in greeting. 'Welcome stranger. I am Fionn and these are my companions and friends.'

'A poor bunch fit only for hunting rabbits and swine,' the stranger growled and, with that, he tore off his helmet and threw it at Fionn's feet. 'I challenge your best runner to a contest—the winner to take the gold, chariots, horses and dogs of the Fianna.'

Silence followed this unexpected demand. Only the beggarman was unabashed. ''Tis the challenge I'm waiting for,' he chortled. ''Tis the race I'll run.' No one paid the slightest attention to what he was saying.

Conan Maol was the first to recover his wits. He stooped down to pick up the helmet, but was tripped by the beggarman.

'Why did you do that, you looderamaun?' he howled. 'Why did you trip me with your big spaugs? A challenge must be taken up.'

'Of course and certainly and by all means,' the beggarman said airily, and before anyone could move hand or foot he had turned a somersault and come up with the helmet firmly fixed on his head.

'I accept the challenge,' he grinned. Then, as if the exertion was altogether too much, he dropped on the sand, put the helmet over his face and began to snore.

Fionn thought it time to take a hand. He picked up the helmet and handed it to the stranger. He was keeping a tight rein on his temper. 'Caelte Mac Ronan is our champion. He will accept your challenge.'

'He can outrun the wind,' Conan boasted.

'He is faster than the deer,' the youth echoed.

'He leaves the swallow behind,' someone else added.

The stranger let out a roar. 'He will not be asked to outrun either the wind, the swallow or the deer. The challenge is that he outruns me. Produce your champion and let us be off.'

Fionn silently counted up to ten. Then he explained. 'Caelte is on his way to Tara to tell the High King we shall spend the night with him. If you will agree to come hunting with us today, to-morrow I promise you a good contest.'

'The race will take place when and where I decide,' the stranger bullied. 'And that is now. This very minute.'

Fionn chewed his thumb and made a silent wish. 'Let me make the right decision. Let me pick someone who can beat this arrogant stranger.'

'That someone is me,' the beggarman whispered in Fionn's ear.

Because Fionn had made his wish at the right moment, he knew what his answer was. He put an arm on the beggarman's shoulder. 'Our friend here will take up the challenge.'

Conan Maol could scarcely believe his ears. He looked at Fionn in disgust. 'Would you let Forty Coats disgrace us before the world?' he stormed.

'We'll never lift our heads again,' the youth wailed.

'Until the end of doom,' the stranger bellowed. 'I will not move a foot to race a great clumsy clod of a beggarman. Let bald head race me if no one else will,' and he gave Conan a push that sent him tumbling into the sea.

How it happened, and it happened quickly, no one knew, but next, the stranger had measured his length on the sand and the beggarman was standing with one great, broken boot on the stranger's head.

'You'll race me,' he was saying softly. 'You'll accept my offer or I'll kick you and your boat to the end of the world. What length had you in mind?'

The stranger choked with rage, but managed to get out: 'I never run less than sixty miles.'

'A small trot I frequently take before breakfast,' and the beggarman grinned, showing one black tooth. 'From this place to the Hill of Rushes—Slieve Luachra—is exactly sixty miles. If Fionn will kindly lend us two of his noble horses we shall ride there in style and race back on foot. Will that suit, dear heart?' and he rolled the stranger over on his face.

'I don't care how it's done,' the stranger snarled, spitting out sand.

It took ten of the Fianna to hoist the beggarman on to the saddle while the stranger moodily waited, kicking his heels. Then they were off.

For the length of the day they travelled through Leinster and down into Munster, overtaking herds of mighty deer and careering bronze chariots. They passed striking palaces guarded by warriors with purple cloaks and golden bracelets and who carried shields and five-pronged spears. In all the land there was no fence or stone wall, only wide plains, sweet with garlic, primrose and slender fern. Mostly the beggarman sang in a cracked voice and sometimes he slept, but the stranger rode grim-faced and never uttered a word.

At length and at long last they reached Slieve Luachra and here they dismounted. Immediately the horses were free they tossed their manes and went racing back to where the Fianna waited at Binn Eadair.

Night clouds were gathering up and a cold wind whipped the trees, making them shiver.

'My bones are growing old,' the beggarman wheezed. 'A night in the open would be the death of me. I think we had better build a shelter to pass the night.'

The stranger looked at his companion as if he had as many heads as coats. 'You must be raving mad.'

The beggarman chuckled. 'Say no more. I'll build a little house myself, but if you won't help you won't share.' He began running around, pulling up trees as if they were rushes, and in no time at all he had built a timbered, well-thatched house and a splendid fire.

He cocked an eye at the stranger who was crouched on a log of wood. 'Now I have a grand fire going, it's a pity we haven't some food. Will you help me search?'

'Search by yourself,' roared the stranger beside himself with rage. 'And if a boar attacks you I shan't lift a finger to help.'

'Then houseless and supperless you shall be this very night,' the beggarman sighed. Wagging his head, he disappeared into the wood. When he returned, he had a fine, fat pig over his shoulder and the crackling and sizzling and smell of delicious roast pork soon filled the house and was wafted outside to madden the stranger with hunger.

When the beggarman had finished eating he made himself a bed of soft rushes beside the fire and before long he was deep in sleep, though the noise of his snores shook the house, sent the rushes whistling and kept the stranger awake for most of the night.

The sun was shining over the hill when the beggarman awoke to find two angry eyes staring down at him. 'Wake up,' the stranger hissed, tugging the beggarman's beard. 'Get up, you lazy good-for-nothing, if we are ever to begin the race.'

'I never get up till I have my fill of sleep and there is another hour or two due to me,' the beggarman grumbled. 'If you are in such a hurry, start running now and I'll trot in your tracks when I'm properly awake.'

When next the beggarman opened his eyes, the sun was high in the heavens and a stray goat was nuzzling him gently. He yawned, got up, milked the goat and finished the remains of last night's supper. Then he tied the pork bones in the tail of his coat and set off.

Not a doubt about it but he ran in a most contorted manner. He twisted his hairy legs, spattered with mud, and when he jumped, his coat tails flapped in the wind behind him. He ran in leaps and jumps, spurts and stops. Sometimes he ran backwards and a lot of the time he ran sideways, but for all that, he covered a fair amount of ground.

Half-way to Binn Eadair he caught up with the stranger who was running well with his head back, his fists up, and his feet going so hard that they couldn't be seen for dust.

'I saved you some breakfast, pulse of my heart,' the beggarman chortled, pulling the bones out of his coat tail. 'They will give you strength to run.'

'Keep your dirty scraps,' the stranger panted. 'I'd sooner starve than eat your leavings.'

'Why don't you exert yourself a little?' the beggarman coaxed. 'Why don't you make an effort to win the race?'

'Try running like this,' the beggarman besought him, and gave such a leap that he was over the hill and into the next valley before he came down to earth again.

Here the hedges were thick with blackberries and the beggarman slowed down to a canter, then a trot and finally came to a full stop.

'I'm woefully hungry,' he sighed, 'and I'm dying of thirst and, surely, eating is better than running.' He picked a berry and then another and next he was cramming handfuls into his mouth. When the stranger arrived, the beggarman was stripping the bushes bare, and his mouth, his hands and all of his forty coats were stained with purple juice.

'Who lost the tails of his coat?' the stranger sneered, slowing down. He was rather glad to draw breath.

'I never speak with my mouth full,' the beggarman mumbled haughtily. 'Besides which I don't much care for riddles.'

'Your tails are caught in a bush ten miles back,' the stranger announced nastily, 'and the stench and the horrid sight are scaring the birds away.'

The beggarman sighed. 'Oh dear, I'd best go back. I don't like to upset my feathered friends.' He wiped his mouth with his sleeve. 'Let you stay here and refresh yourself, dear heart, and I'll join you when I have my tails back for I'm not half finished yet.'

'Not a minute will I wait,' screeched the stranger. 'Not even half a second.' He was so keen to be off that he tripped over himself, bumped into a blackberry bush and frightened a highly-strung sparrow.

The beggarman ran backwards and when at last he found the bush he recovered his coat tails and tied them on. Then he took two jumps that landed him back where he was at the blackberry hedge.

He ate and ate until he could eat no more. After that, he took off his topcoat, made a bundle and stuffed the pockets, the sleeves and the lining with blackberries.

'Now I have the strength back I must put some spring into my feet,' he told himself firmly and swinging the bundles over his shoulder he began to run. He went with such speed that trees blew down and strong animals trembled for their lives.

On top of Binn Eadair, Fionn and the Fianna were gathered. All that day they had discussed every aspect of the race, the out-rageousness of the stranger, the madness of Fionn to pick on the beggarman and what would happen if the race were lost. Then they were silent for there was no more to be said and evening was drawing to a close.

'I see a speck of dirt,' Fionn called out at last.

'I hear a trample,' shouted Conan Maol, not to be out-done.

'I spy a man carrying something,' said the youth, who had sharp sight. 'It's the stranger and he's carrying the beggarman on his back.'

'The great, lazy, slobbering hulk,' Conan Maol wailed.

'The useless, good-for-nothing vagabond,' the youth added for good measure.

'Oh why wasn't I let run the race?' Conan Maol moaned.

'Wait,' said Fionn and he screwed up his eyes until the tears ran down his face. 'It's the beggarman with a sack on his back and far behind him, losing ground, is the stranger.'

At this the Fianna let out a great shout of joy and went galloping and rolling and jumping down the hill to the strand, cheering and thumping and walloping each other with sheer relief.

They tried to lift the beggarman shoulder high, but he was emptying out his sack of blackberries and crushing them into the sand.

'Food to fill my gullet and the crevices of my stomach,' he cried and began cramming the purple mass into his mouth.

While they stood and stared, a tiny figure that grew larger and which turned out to be the stranger came running up. His sword was drawn and his face contorted with fury. He made a lunge at the beggarman and was knocked aside by a ball of blackberry mess that seemed to come out of nowhere. When they looked again the beggarman was wiping his hands in the tail of his coat and the stranger's head had toppled off his shoulders and was bouncing about like a football.

'I'd best do the decent thing,' the beggarman muttered. 'Sure, my heart is as soft as butter.' He picked up the head and flung it back where it stuck on back to front. The last they saw of the stranger he was running across the beach towards his boat, his feet pointing towards the sea and his face grimacing back at them.

Conan Maol cleared his throat and said gruffly: 'All the same, I feel sorry for the stranger. Now he'll never know what way to go.'

Fionn clapped him on the shoulder. 'Save your pity. The stranger is a powerful magician with more tricks than the beggarman has coats.'

'Maybe so, but the last trick is mine,' the beggarman chuckled and he threw a hairy leg over a goat that had wandered down the hill.

As he straightened up, the years fell away and his forty coats were now a magnificent cloak of many colours.

'Farewell, Fionn and the Fianna,' he called, and his voice was clear water running, bells chiming, wind calling. 'I am a prince of the Shee of Rath Cruachan in the Land of the Ever Young. Once a year, on November Eve, I take the form of a mortal. I've saved the honour of the Fianna and I'll ride home in style.'

The goat's ragged fur had turned silkily smooth and the horns gleamed like silver. For a moment the animal stood poised against the skyline, then raised its massive head towards the sea and went running across the sands and over the waves.

The Fianna raised their arms in a farewell salute, and then both goat and rider were lost in the white sea-mist.

10

The Story Of Uncle Silas

SHERIDAN LE FANU

Maud Ruthyn, a lonely young heiress, has been made a ward of 'Uncle Silas' under the terms of her father's Will. Uncle Silas, a mysterious character, already suspected of one murder, would be the first to profit by his niece's death. Maud's cousin, Monica, Lady Knollys, confesses: 'I don't understand metaphysics, my dear, nor witchcraft. I sometimes believe in the supernatural, and sometimes I don't. Silas Ruthyn is himself alone, and I can't define him, because I don't understand him. Perhaps other souls than humans are sometimes born into the world and clothed in flesh.'

And so it was like the yelling of phantom hounds and hunters, and the thunder of their coursers in the air—a furious, grand, and supernatural music, which in my fancy made a suitable accompaniment to the discussion of that enigmatical person—martyr—angel —demon—Uncle Silas—with whom my fate was now so strangely linked, and whom I had begun to fear.

'The storm blows from that point,' I said, indicating it with my hand and eye, although the window shutters and curtains were closed, 'I saw all the trees bend that way this evening. That way stands the great lonely wood, where my darling father and mother lie. Oh, how dreadful on nights like this, to think of them—a vault!—damp, and dark and solitary—under the storm.'

Cousin Monica Knollys looked wistfully in the same direction, and with a short sigh she said:

'We think too much of the poor remains, and too little of the
spirit which lives for ever. I am sure they are happy.' And she
sighed again. 'I wish I dare hope as confidently for myself. Yes,
Maud, it is sad. We are such materialists, we can't help feeling so.
We forget how well it is for us that our present bodies are not to
last always. They are constructed for a time and place of trouble—
plainly mere temporary machines that wear out, constantly
exhibiting failure and decay, and with such tremendous capacity
for pain. The body lies alone, and so it ought, for it is plainly its
good Creator's will; it is only the tabernacle, not the person, who
is clothed upon after death, Saint Paul says, "with a house which
is from heaven". So Maud, darling, although the thought will
trouble us again and again, there is nothing in it; and the poor
mortal body is only the cold ruin of a habitation which *they* have
forsaken before we do. So this great wind, you say, is blowing
towards us from the wood there. If so, Maud, it is blowing from
Bartram-Haugh, too, over the trees and chimneys of that old
place, and the mysterious old man, who is quite right in thinking
I don't like him; and I can fancy him an old enchanter in his castle,
waving his familiar spirits on the wind to fetch and carry tidings
of our occupations here.'

I lifted up my head and listened to the storm, dying away in the
distance sometimes—sometimes swelling and pealing around and
above us—and through the dark and solitude my thoughts sped
away to Bartram-Haugh and Uncle Silas.

'This letter,' I said at last, 'makes me feel differently. I think he
is a stern old man—is he?'

'It is twenty years now since I saw him,' answered Lady
Knollys. 'I did not choose to visit at his house.'

'Was that before the dreadful occurrence at Bartram-Haugh?'

'Yes—before, dear. He was not a reformed rake, but only a
ruined one then. Austin was very good to him. Mr Danvers says
it is quite unaccountable how Silas can have made away with the
immense sums he got from his brother from time to time without
benefiting himself in the least. But, my dear, he played*; and
trying to help a man who plays, and is unlucky—and some men
are, I believe, habitually unlucky—is like trying to fill a vessel that
has no bottom. I think, by the by, my hopeful nephew, Charles
Oakely, plays. Then Silas went most unjustifiably into all manner

* at cards; gambled.

of speculations, and your poor father had to pay everything. He lost something quite astounding in that bank that ruined so many country gentlemen—poor Sir Harry Shackleton, in Yorkshire, had to sell half his estate. But your kind father went on helping him, up to his marriage—I mean in that extravagant way which was really totally useless.'

'Has my aunt been long dead?'

'Twelve or fifteen years—more, indeed—she died before your poor mamma. She was very unhappy, and I am sure would have given her right hand she had never married Silas.'

'Did you like her?'

'No, dear; she was a coarse, vulgar woman.'

'Coarse and vulgar, and Uncle Silas's wife!' I echoed in extreme surprise, for Uncle Silas was a man of fashion—a beau in his day—and might have married women of good birth and fortune, I had no doubt, and so I expressed myself.

'Yes, dear; so he might, and poor dear Austin was very anxious he should, and would have helped him with a handsome settlement, I dare say, but he chose to marry the daughter of a Denbigh innkeeper.'

'How utterly incredible!' I exclaimed.

'Not the least incredible, dear—a kind of thing not at all so uncommon as you fancy.'

'What!—a gentleman of fashion and refinement marry a person——'

'A barmaid!—just so,' said Lady Knollys. 'I think I could count half a dozen men of fashion who, to my knowledge, have ruined themselves just in a similar way.'

'Well, at all events, it must be allowed that in this he proved himself altogether unworldly.'

'Not a bit unworldly, but very vicious,' replied Cousin Monica, with a careless little laugh. 'She was very beautiful, curiously beautiful, for a person in her station. She was very like that Lady Hamilton who was Nelson's sorceress—elegantly beautiful, but perfectly low and stupid. I believe, to do him justice, he only intended to ruin her; but she was cunning enough to insist upon marriage. Men who have never in all their lives denied themselves the indulgence of a single fancy, cost what it may, will not be baulked even by that condition if the *penchant* be only violent enough.'

I did not half understand this piece of worldly psychology, at which Lady Knollys seemed to laugh.

'Poor Silas, certainly he struggled honestly against the consequences, for he tried after the honeymoon to prove the marriage bad. But the Welsh parson and the innkeeper papa were too strong for him, and the young lady was able to hold her struggling swain fast in that respectable noose—and a pretty prize he proved!'

'And she died, poor thing, broken-hearted, I heard.'

'She died, at all events, about ten years after her marriage; but I really can't say about her heart. She certainly had enough ill-usage, I believe, to kill her; but I don't know that she had feeling enough to die of it, if it had not been that she drank: I am told that Welsh women often do. There was jealousy, of course, and brutal quarrelling, and all sorts of horrid stories. I visited at Bartram-Haugh for a year or two, though no one else would. But when that sort of thing began, of course I gave it up; it was out of the question. I don't think poor Austin ever knew how bad it was. And then came that odious business about wretched Mr Charke. You know he—he committed suicide at Bartram.'

'I never heard about that,' I said; and we both paused, and she looked sternly at the fire, and the storm roared and ha-ha-ed till the old house shook again.

'But Uncle Silas could not help that,' I said at last.

'No, he could not help it,' she acquiesced unpleasantly.

'And Uncle Silas was ——' I paused in a sort of fear.

'He was suspected by some people of having killed him'—she completed the sentence.

There was another long pause here, during which the storm outside bellowed and hooted like an angry mob roaring at the windows for a victim. An intolerable and sickening sensation overpowered me.

'But *you* did not suspect him, Cousin Knollys?' I said, trembling very much.

'No,' she answered very sharply. 'I told you so before. Of course I did not.'

There was another silence.

'I wish, Cousin Monica,' I said, drawing close to her, 'you had not said *that* about Uncle Silas being like a wizard, and sending his spirits on the wind to listen. But I'm very glad you never suspected him.' I insinuated my cold hand into hers, and looked

into her face I know not with what expression. She looked down
into mine with a hard, haughty stare, I thought.

'Of *course* I never suspected him; and *never* ask me *that* question
again, Maud Ruthyn.'

Was it family pride, or what was it, that gleamed so fiercely
from her eyes as she said this? I was frightened—I was wounded—
I burst into tears.

'What is my darling crying for? I did not mean to be cross.
Was I cross?' said this momentary phantom of a grim Lady
Knollys, in an instant translated again into kind, pleasant Cousin
Monica, with her arms about my neck.

'No, no, indeed—only I thought I had vexed you; and, I
believe, thinking of Uncle Silas makes me nervous, and I can't help
thinking of him nearly always.'

'Nor can I, although we might both easily find something
better to think of. Suppose we try?' said Lady Knollys.

'But, first, I must know a little more about that Mr Charke,
and what circumstances enabled Uncle Silas's enemies to found on
his death that wicked slander, which has done no one any good,
and caused some persons so much misery. There is Uncle Silas,
I may say, ruined by it; and we all know how it darkened the life
of my dear father.'

'People will talk, my dear. Your Uncle Silas had injured himself
before that in the opinion of the people of his county. He was a
black sheep, in fact. Very bad stories were told and believed of
him. His marriage certainly was a disadvantage, you know, and
the miserable scenes that went on in his disreputable house—all
that predisposed people to believe ill of him.'

'How long is it since it happened?'

'Oh, a long time; I think before you were born,' answered she.

'And the injustice still lives—they have not forgotten it yet?'
said I, for such a period appeared to me long enough to have
consigned anything in its nature perishable to oblivion.

Lady Knollys smiled.

'Tell me, like a darling cousin, the whole story as well as you
can recollect it. Who was Mr Charke?'

'Mr Charke, my dear, was a gentleman of the turf—that is the
phrase, I think—one of those London men, without birth or
breeding, who merely in right of their vices and their money are
admitted to associate with young dandies who like hounds and
horses, and all that sort of thing. That set knew him very well,

but of course no one else. He was at the Matlock races, and your uncle asked him to Bartram-Haugh; and the creature, Jew or Gentile, whatever he was, fancied there was more honour than, perhaps, there really was in a visit to Bartram-Haugh.'

'For the kind of person you describe, it *was*, I think, a rather unusual honour to be invited to stay in the house of a man of Uncle Ruthyn's birth.'

'Well, so it was perhaps; for though they knew him very well on the course, and would ask him to their tavern dinners, they would not, of course, admit him to the houses where ladies were. But Silas's wife was not much regarded at Bartram-Haugh. Indeed, she was very little seen, for she was every evening tipsy in her bedroom, poor woman!'

'How miserable!' I exclaimed.

'I don't think it troubled Silas very much, for she drank gin, they said, poor thing, and the expense was not much; and, on the whole, I really think he was glad she drank, for it kept her out of his way, and was likely to kill her. At this time your poor father, who was thoroughly disgusted at his marriage, had stopped the supplies, you know, and Silas was very poor, and as hungry as a hawk, and they said he pounced upon this rich London gamester, intending to win his money. I am telling you now all that was said afterwards. The races lasted I forget how many days, and Mr Charke stayed at Bartram-Haugh all this time and for some days after. It was thought that poor Austin would pay all Silas's gambling debts, and so this wretched Mr Charke made heavy wagers with him on the races, and they played very deep, besides, at Bartram. He and Silas used to sit up at night at cards. All these particulars, as I told you, came out afterwards, for there was an inquest, you know, and then Silas published what he called his "statement", and there was a great deal of most distressing correspondence in the newspapers.'

'And why did Mr Charke kill himself?' I asked.

'Well, I will tell you first what all are agreed about. The second night after the races, your uncle and Mr Charke sat up till between two and three o'clock in the morning, quite by themselves, in the parlour. Mr Charke's servant was at the Stag's Head Inn at Feltram, and therefore could throw no light upon what occurred at night at Bartram-Haugh; but he was there at six o'clock in the morning, and very early at his master's door by his direction. He had locked it, as was his habit, upon the inside, and the key was in

the lock, which turned out afterwards a very important point.
On knocking he found that he could not awaken his master,
because, as it appeared when the door was forced open, his master
was lying dead at his bedside . . . as they described it, with his
throat cut.'

'How horrible!' cried I.

'So it was. Your uncle Silas was called up, and greatly shocked
of course, and he did what I believe was best. He had everything
left as nearly as possible in the exact state in which it had been
found, and he sent his own servant forthwith for the coroner and,
being himself a justice of the peace, he took the depositions of
Mr Charke's servant while all the incidents were still fresh in his
memory.'

'Could anything be more straightforward, more right and
wise?' I said.

'Oh, nothing of course,' answered Lady Knollys, I thought a
little dryly.

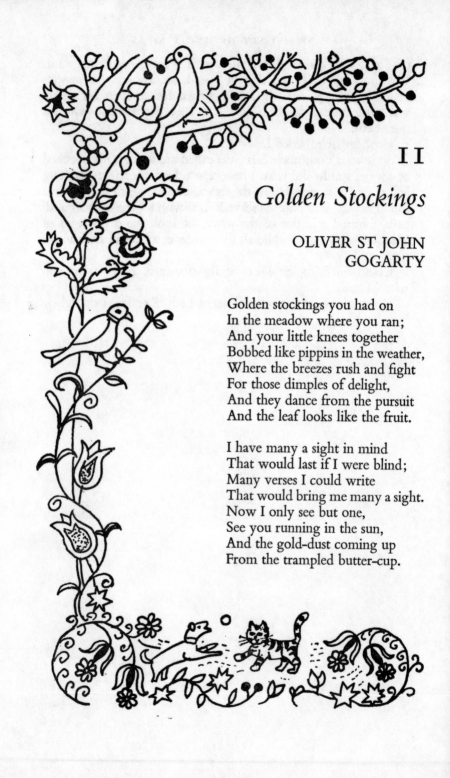

II

Golden Stockings

OLIVER ST JOHN
GOGARTY

Golden stockings you had on
In the meadow where you ran;
And your little knees together
Bobbed like pippins in the weather,
Where the breezes rush and fight
For those dimples of delight,
And they dance from the pursuit
And the leaf looks like the fruit.

I have many a sight in mind
That would last if I were blind;
Many verses I could write
That would bring me many a sight.
Now I only see but one,
See you running in the sun,
And the gold-dust coming up
From the trampled butter-cup.

12

The Happy Prince

OSCAR WILDE

High above the city, on a tall column, stood the statue of the Happy Prince. He was gilded all over with thin leaves of fine gold, for eyes he had two bright sapphires, and a large red ruby glowed on his sword-hilt.

He was very much admired indeed. 'He is as beautiful as a weathercock,' remarked one of the Town Councillors who wished to gain a reputation for having artistic tastes; 'only not quite so useful,' he added, fearing lest people should think him unpractical, which he really was not.

'Why can't you be like the Happy Prince?' asked a sensible mother of her little boy who was crying for the moon. 'The Happy Prince never dreams of crying for anything.'

'I am glad there is someone in the world who is quite happy,' muttered a disappointed man as he gazed at the wonderful statue.

'He looks just like an angel,' said the Charity Children as they came out of the cathedral in their bright scarlet cloaks and their clean white pinafores.

'How do you know?' said the Mathematical Master. 'You have never seen one.'

'Ah! but we have, in our dreams,' answered the children: and the Mathematical Master frowned and looked very severe, for he did not approve of children dreaming.

One night there flew over the city a little Swallow. His friends had gone away to Egypt six weeks before, but he had stayed behind, for he was in love with the most beautiful Reed. He had met her early in the spring as he was flying down the river after a big yellow moth, and had been so attracted by her slender waist that he had stopped to talk to her.

'Shall I love you?' said the Swallow, who liked to come to the point at once, and the Reed made him a low bow. So he flew round and round her, touching the water with his wings, and making silver ripples. This was his courtship, and it lasted all through the summer.

'It is a ridiculous attachment,' twittered the other Swallows. 'She has no money, and far too many relations'; and indeed the river was quite full of Reeds. Then, when the autumn came, they all flew away.

After they had gone he felt lonely, and began to tire of his lady-love. 'She has no conversation,' he said, 'and I am afraid that she is a coquette, for she is always flirting with the wind.' And certainly, whenever the wind blew, the Reed made the most graceful curtseys. 'I admit that she is domestic,' he continued, 'but I love travelling, and my wife, consequently, should love travelling also.'

'Will you come away with me?' he said finally to her, but the Reed shook her head, she was so attached to her home.

'You have been trifling with me,' he cried, 'I am off to the Pyramids. Good-bye!' and he flew away.

All day long he flew, and at night-time he arrived at the city. 'Where shall I put up?' he said. 'I hope the town has made preparations.'

Then he saw the statue on the tall column.

'I will put up there,' he cried: 'it is a fine position with plenty of fresh air.' So he alighted just between the feet of the Happy Prince.

'I have a golden bedroom,' he said softly to himself as he looked round, and he prepared to go to sleep; but just as he was putting his head under his wing a large drop of water fell on him.

'What a curious thing!' he cried: 'there is not a single cloud in the sky, the stars are quite clear and bright, and yet it is raining. The climate in the north of Europe is really dreadful. The Reed used to like the rain, but that was merely her selfishness.'

Then another drop fell.

'What is the use of a statue if it cannot keep the rain off?' he

said. 'I must look for a good chimney-pot,' and he determined to
fly away.

But before he had opened his wings, a third drop fell, and he
looked up and saw—Ah! what did he see?

The eyes of the Happy Prince were filled with tears, and tears
were running down his golden cheeks. His face was so beautiful
in the moonlight that the little Swallow was filled with pity.

'Who are you?' he said.

'I am the Happy Prince.'

'Why are you weeping then?' asked the Swallow: 'you have
quite drenched me.'

'When I was alive and had a human heart,' answered the statue,
'I did not know what tears were, for I lived in the Palace of
Sans-Souci, where sorrow is not allowed to enter. In the daytime
I played with my companions in the garden, and in the evening I
led the dance in the Great Hall. Round the garden ran a very lofty
wall, but I never cared to ask what lay beyond it, everything about
me was so beautiful. My courtiers called me the Happy Prince
and happy indeed I was, if pleasure be happiness. So I lived, and so
I died. And now that I am dead they have set me up here so high
that I can see all the ugliness and all the misery of my city,
and though my heart is made of lead yet I cannot choose but
weep.'

'What! is he not of solid gold?' said the Swallow to himself.
He was far too polite to make any personal remarks out loud.

'Far away,' continued the statue in a low musical voice, 'far
away in a little street there is a poor house. One of the windows is
open, and through it I can see a woman seated at a table. Her face
is thin and worn, and she has coarse, red hands, all pricked by the
needle, for she is a seamstress. She is embroidering passion-flowers
on a satin gown for the loveliest of the Queen's maids-of-honour
to wear at the next Court-ball. In a bed in the corner of the room
her little boy is lying ill. He has a fever and is asking for oranges.
His mother has nothing to give him but river water, so he is
crying. Swallow, Swallow, little Swallow, will you not bring her
the ruby out of my sword-hilt? My feet are fastened to this
pedestal and I cannot move.'

'I am waited for in Egypt,' said the Swallow. 'My friends are
flying up and down the Nile, and talking to the large lotus-
flowers. Soon they will go to sleep in the tomb of the great King.
The King is there himself in his painted coffin. He is wrapped in

yellow linen, and embalmed with spices. Round his neck is a chain of pale green jade, and his hands are like withered leaves.'

'Swallow, Swallow, little Swallow,' said the Prince, 'will you not stay with me for one night, and be my messenger? The boy is so thirsty, and the mother so sad.'

'I don't think I like boys,' answered the Swallow. 'Last summer, when I was staying on the river, there were two rude boys, the miller's sons, who were always throwing stones at me. They never hit me, of course; we swallows fly far too well for that, and besides I come of a family famous for its agility; but still, it was a mark of disrespect.'

But the Happy Prince looked so sad that the little Swallow was sorry. 'It is very cold here,' he said, 'but I will stay with you for one night, and be your messenger.'

'Thank you, little Swallow,' said the Prince.

So the Swallow picked out the great ruby from the Prince's sword, and flew away with it in his beak over the roofs of the town.

He passed by the cathedral tower, where the white marble angels were sculptured. He passed by the palace and heard the sound of dancing. A beautiful girl came out on the balcony with her lover. 'How wonderful the stars are,' he said to her, 'and how wonderful is the power of love.'

'I hope my dress will be ready in time for the State ball,' she answered. 'I have ordered passion-flowers to be embroidered on it; but the seamstresses are so lazy.'

He passed over the river, and saw the lanterns hanging on the masts of the ships. At last he came to the poor house and looked in. The boy was tossing feverishly on his bed, and the mother had fallen asleep, she was so tired. In he hopped, and laid the great ruby on the table beside the woman's thimble. Then he flew gently round the bed, fanning the boy's forehead with his wings. 'How cool I feel!' said the boy, 'I must be getting better'; and he sank into a delicious slumber.

Then the Swallow flew back to the Happy Prince, and told him what he had done. 'It is curious,' he remarked, 'but I feel quite warm now, although it is so cold.'

'That is because you have done a good action,' said the Prince. And the little Swallow began to think, and then he fell asleep. Thinking always made him sleepy.

When day broke he flew down to the river and had a bath.

'What a remarkable phenomenon!' said the Professor of Ornithology as he was passing over the bridge. 'A swallow in winter!' And he wrote a long letter about it to the local newspaper. Everyone quoted it, it was so full of so many words that they could not understand.

'Tonight I go to Egypt,' said the Swallow, and he was in high spirits at the prospect. He visited all the public monuments, and sat a long time on top of the church steeple. Wherever he went the Sparrows chirruped, and said to each other, 'What a distinguished stranger!' so he enjoyed himself very much.

When the moon rose he flew back to the Happy Prince. 'Have you any commissions for Egypt?' he cried. 'I am just starting.'

'Swallow, Swallow, little Swallow,' said the Prince, 'will you not stay with me one night longer?'

'I am waited for in Egypt,' answered the Swallow. 'Tomorrow my friends will fly up to the Second Cataract. The river-horse couches there among the bulrushes, and on a great granite throne sits the God Memnon. All night long he watches the stars, and when the morning star shines he utters one cry of joy, and then he is silent. At noon the yellow lions come down to the water's edge to drink. They have eyes like green beryls, and their roar is louder than the roar of the cataract.'

'Swallow, Swallow, little Swallow,' said the Prince, 'far away across the city I see a young man in a garret. He is leaning over a desk covered with papers, and in a tumbler by his side there is a bunch of withered violets. His hair is brown and crisp and his lips are red as a pomegranate, and he has large and dreamy eyes. He is trying to finish a play for the Director of the Theatre, but he is too cold to write any more. There is no fire in the grate, and hunger has made him faint.'

'I will wait with you one night longer,' said the Swallow, who really had a good heart. 'Shall I take him another ruby?'

'Alas! I have no ruby now,' said the Prince; 'my eyes are all that I have left. They are made of rare sapphires which were brought out of India a thousand years ago. Pluck out one of them, and take it to him. He will sell it to the jeweller, and buy firewood, and finish his play.'

'Dear Prince,' said the Swallow, 'I cannot do that,' and he began to weep.

'Swallow, Swallow, little Swallow,' said the Prince, 'do as I command you.'

So the Swallow plucked out the Prince's eye, and flew away to the student's garret. It was easy enough to get in, as there was a hole in the roof. Through this he darted, and came into the room. The young man had his head buried in his hands, so he did not hear the flutter of the bird's wings, and when he looked up he found the beautiful sapphire lying on the withered violets.

'I am beginning to be appreciated,' he cried. 'This is from some great admirer. Now I can finish my play,' and he looked quite happy.

The next day the Swallow flew down to the harbour. He sat on the mast of a large vessel and watched the sailors hauling big chests out of the hold with ropes. 'Heavea-hoy!' they shouted as each chest came up.

'I am going to Egypt!' cried the Swallow, but nobody minded, and when the moon rose he flew back to the Happy Prince.

'I am come to bid you good-bye,' he cried.

'Swallow, Swallow, little Swallow,' said the Prince, 'will you not stay with me one night longer?'

'It is winter,' answered the Swallow, 'and the chill snow will soon be here. In Egypt the sun is warm on the green palm-trees, and the crocodiles lie in the mud and look lazily about them. My companions are building a nest in the Temple of Baalbec, and the pink and white doves are watching them, and cooing to each other. Dear Prince I must leave you, but I will never forget you, and next spring I will bring you back two beautiful jewels in place of those you have given away. The ruby shall be redder than a red rose, and the sapphire shall be as blue as the great sea.'

'In the square below,' said the Happy Prince, 'there stands a little match-girl. She has let her matches fall in the gutter, and they are all spoiled. Her father will beat her if she does not bring home some money, and she is crying. She has no shoes or stockings, and her little head is bare. Pluck out my other eye, and give it to her, and her father will not beat her.'

'I will stay with you one night longer,' said the Swallow, 'but I cannot pluck out your eye. You would be quite blind then.'

'Swallow, Swallow, little Swallow,' said the Prince, 'do as I command you.'

So he plucked out the Prince's other eye, and darted down with it. He swooped past the match-girl, and slipped the jewel into the palm of her hand. 'What a lovely bit of glass!' cried the little girl; and she ran home, laughing.

Then the Swallow came back to the Prince. 'You are blind now,' he said, 'so I will stay with you always.'

'No, little Swallow,' said the poor Prince, 'you must go away to Egypt.'

'I will stay with you always,' said the Swallow, and he slept at the Prince's feet.

All the next day he sat on the Prince's shoulder, and told him stories of what he had seen in strange lands. He told him of the red ibises, who stand in long rows on the banks of the Nile and catch goldfish in their beaks; of the Sphinx, who is as old as the world itself, and lives in the desert, and knows everything; of the merchants who walk slowly by the side of their camels and carry amber beads in their hands; of the King of the Mountains of the Moon, who is as black as ebony, and worships a large crystal; of the great green snake that sleeps in a palm-tree, and has twenty priests to feed it with honey-cakes; and of the pygmies who sail over a big lake on large flat leaves, and are always at war with the butterflies.

'Dear little Swallow,' said the Prince, 'you tell me of marvellous things, but more marvellous than anything is the suffering of men and of women. There is no Mystery so great as Misery. Fly over my city, little Swallow, and tell me what you see there.'

So the Swallow flew over the great city, and saw the rich making merry in their beautiful houses, while the beggars were sitting at the gates. He flew into dark lanes, and saw the white faces of starving children looking out listlessly at the black streets. Under the archway of a bridge two little boys were lying in one another's arms to try and keep themselves warm.

'How hungry we are!' they said.

'You must not lie here,' shouted the watchman, and they wandered out into the rain.

Then he flew back and told the Prince what he had seen.

'I am covered with fine gold,' said the Prince, 'you must take it off, leaf by leaf, and give it to my poor; the living always think that gold can make them happy.'

Leaf after leaf of the fine gold the Swallow picked off, till the Happy Prince looked quite dull and grey. Leaf after leaf of the fine gold he brought to the poor, and the children's faces grew rosier, and they laughed and played games in the street. 'We have bread now!' they cried.

Then the snow came, and after the snow came the frost. The

streets looked as if they were made of silver, they were so bright
and glistening: long icicles like crystal daggers hung down from
the eaves of the houses, everybody went about in furs, and the
little boys wore scarlet caps and skated on the ice.

The poor little Swallow grew colder and colder, but he would
not leave the Prince, he loved him too well. He picked up crumbs
outside the baker's door when the baker was not looking and
tried to keep himself warm by flapping his wings.

But at last he knew that he was going to die. He had just enough
strength to fly up to the Prince's shoulder once more. 'Good-bye,
dear Prince,' he murmured, 'will you let me kiss your hand?'

'I am glad that you are going to Egypt at last, little Swallow,'
said the Prince, 'you have stayed too long here; but you must kiss
me on the lips, for I love you.'

'It is not to Egypt that I am going,' said the Swallow. 'I am
going to the House of Death. Death is the brother of Sleep, is he
not?'

And he kissed the Happy Prince on the lips and fell down dead
at his feet. At that moment a curious crack sounded inside the
statue as if something had broken. The fact is that the leaden
heart had snapped right in two. It certainly was a dreadfully hard
frost.

Early the next morning the Mayor was walking in the square
below in company with the Town Councillors. As they passed
the column he looked up at the statue: 'Dear me! how shabby the
Happy Prince looks!' he said.

'How shabby, indeed,' cried the Town Councillors, who always
agreed with the Mayor: and they went up to look at it.

'The ruby has fallen out of his sword, his eyes are gone, and he
is golden no longer,' said the Mayor, 'in fact he is little better than
a beggar!'

'Little better than a beggar,' said the Town Councillors.

'And here is actually a dead bird at his feet!' continued the
Mayor. 'We must really issue a proclamation that birds are not
to be allowed to die here.' And the Town Clerk made a note of
the suggestion.

So they pulled down the statue of the Happy Prince. 'As he is
no longer beautiful he is no longer useful,' said the Art Professor
at the University.

Then they melted the statue in a furnace, and the Mayor held a meeting of the Corporation to decide what was to be done with the metal.

'We must have another statue, of course,' he said, 'and it shall be a statue of myself.'

'Of myself,' said each of the Town Councillors, and they quarrelled. When I last heard of them they were quarrelling still.

'What a strange thing!' said the overseer of the workmen at the foundry. 'This broken lead heart will not melt in the furnace. We must throw it away.' So they threw it on a dust-heap where the dead Swallow was also lying.

'Bring me the two most precious things in the city,' said God to one of His Angels; and the Angel brought Him the leaden heart and the dead bird.

'You have rightly chosen,' said God, 'for in my garden of Paradise this little bird shall sing for evermore and in my city of gold the Happy Prince shall praise Me.'

13

The Wounded Cormorant

LIAM O'FLAHERTY

Beneath the great grey cliff of Clogher Mor there was a massive square black rock, dotted with white limpets, sitting in the sea. The sea rose and fell about it frothing. Rising, the sea hoisted the seaweed that grew along the rock's rims until the long red winding strands spread like streams of blood through the white foam. Falling, the tide sucked the strands down taut from their bulbous roots.

Silence. It was noon. The sea was calm. Rock-birds slept on its surface, their beaks resting on their fat white breasts. Tall seagulls standing on one leg dozed high up in the ledges of the cliff. On the great rock there was a flock of black cormorants resting, bobbing their long necks to draw the food from their swollen gullets.

Above on the cliff-top a yellow goat was looking down into the sea. She suddenly took fright. She snorted and turned towards the crag at a smart run. Turning, her hoof loosed a flat stone from the cliff's edge. The stone fell, whirling, on to the rock where the cormorants rested. It fell among them with a crash and arose in fragments. The birds swooped into the air. As they rose a fragment of the stone struck one of them in the right leg. The leg was broken. The wounded bird uttered a shrill scream and dropped the leg. As the bird flew outwards from the rock the leg dangled crookedly.

The flock of cormorants did not fly far. As soon as they passed the edge of the rock they dived headlong into the sea. Their long black bodies, with outstretched necks, passed rapidly beneath the surface of the waves, a long way, before they rose again, shaking the brine from their heads. Then they sat in the sea, their black backs shimmering in the sunlight, their pale brown throats thrust forward, their tiny heads poised on their curved long necks. They sat watching, like upright snakes, trying to discover whether there were any enemies near. Seeing nothing, they began to cackle and flutter their feathers.

But the wounded one rushed about in the water flapping its wings in agony. The salt brine stung the wound, and it could not stand still. After a few moments it rose from the sea and set off at a terrific rate, flying along the face of the cliff, mad with pain. It circled the face of the cliff three times, flying in enormous arcs, as if it were trying to flee from the pain in its leg. Then it swooped down again towards the flock and alighted in the water beside them.

The other birds noticed it and began to cackle. It swam close to one bird, but that bird shrieked and darted away from it. It approached another bird, and that bird prodded it viciously with its beak. Then all the birds screamed simultaneously and rose from the water, with a great swish of their long wings. The wounded one rose with them. They flew up to the rock again and alighted on it, bobbing their necks anxiously and peering in all directions, still slightly terrified by the stone that had fallen there. The wounded one alighted on the rocks with them, tried to stand up, and immediately fell on its stomach. But it struggled up again and stood on its unwounded leg.

The other birds, having assured themselves that there was no enemy near, began to look at the wounded one suspiciously. It had its eyes closed, and it was wobbling unstably on its leg. They saw the wounded leg hanging crookedly from its belly and its wings trailing slightly. They began to make curious screaming noises. One bird trotted over to the wounded one and pecked at it. The wounded bird uttered a low scream and fell forward on its chest. It spread out its wings, turned up its beak, and opened it out wide, like a young bird in a nest demanding food.

Immediately the whole flock raised a cackle again and took to their wings. They flew out to sea, high up in the air. The wounded bird struggled up and also took flight after them. But they were far ahead of it, and it could not catch up with them on account of its waning strength. However, they soon wheeled inwards towards the cliff, and it wheeled in after them, all flying low over the water's surface. Then the flock rose slowly, fighting the air fiercely with their long thin wings in order to propel their heavy bodies upwards. They flew half-way up the face of the cliff and alighted on a wide ledge that was dotted with little black pools and white feathers strewn about.

The wounded bird tried to rise too, but it had not gone out to sea far enough in its swoop. Therefore it had not gathered sufficient speed to carry it up to the ledge. It breasted the cliff ten yards below the ledge, and being unable to rise upwards by banking, it had to wheel outwards again, cackling wildly. It flew out very far, descending to the surface of the sea until the tips of its wings touched the water. Then it wheeled inwards once more, rising gradually, making a tremendous effort to gather enough speed to take it to the ledge where its comrades rested. At all costs it must reach them or perish. Cast out from the flock, death was certain. Seagulls would devour it.

When the other birds saw it coming towards them and heard the sharp whirring of its wings as it rose strongly, they began to cackle fiercely, and came in a close line to the brink of the ledge, darting their beaks forward and shivering. The approaching bird cackled also and came headlong at them. It flopped on to the ledge over their backs and screamed, lying on the rock helplessly with its wings spread out, quite exhausted. But they had no mercy. They fell upon it fiercely, tearing at its body with their beaks, plucking out its black feathers and rooting it about with their feet. It struggled madly to creep in farther on the ledge, trying to get into a dark crevice in the cliff to hide, but they dragged it back again and pushed it towards the brink of the ledge. One bird prodded its right eye with its beak. Another gripped the broken leg firmly in its beak and tore at it.

At last the wounded bird lay on its side and began to tremble, offering no resistance to their attacks. Then they cackled loudly, and, dragging it to the brink of the ledge, they hurled it down. It fell, fluttering feebly through the air, slowly descending, turning round and round, closing and opening its wings, until it reached the sea.

Then it fluttered its wings twice and lay still. An advancing wave dashed it against the side of the black rock and then it disappeared, sucked down among the seaweed strands.

14

Weep For Our Pride

JAMES PLUNKETT

The door of the classroom was opened by Mr O'Rourke just as
Brother Quinlan was about to open it to leave. They were both
surprised and said 'Good morning' to one another as they met in
the doorway. Mr O'Rourke, although he met Brother Quinlan
every morning of his life, gave an expansive but oddly unreal
smile and shouted his good morning with bloodcurdling cordial-
ity. They then withdrew to the passage outside to hold a conversation.

In the interval English Poetry books were opened and the class
began to repeat lines. They had been given the whole of a poem
called *Lament for the Death of Eoghan Roe* to learn. It was very
patriotic and dealt with the poisoning of Eoghan Roe by the
accursed English, and the lines were very long, which made it
difficult. The class hated the English for poisoning Eoghan Roe
because the lines about it were so long. What made it worse was
that it was the sort of poem Mr O'Rourke loved. If it was *Hail to
thee blythe spirit* he wouldn't be so fond of it. But he could declaim
this one for them in a rich, fruity, provincial baritone and would
knock hell out of anybody who had not learned it.

Peter had not learned it. Realizing how few were the minutes
left to him he ran his eyes over stanza after stanza and began to
murmur fragments from each in hopeless desperation. Swaine,
who sat beside him, said, 'Do you know this?'

'No,' Peter said, 'I haven't even looked at it.'

'My God,' Swaine breathed in horror, 'you'll be mangled.'

'You could give us a prompt.'

'And be torn limb from limb,' said Swaine with conviction; 'not likely.'

Peter closed his eyes. It was all his mother's fault. He had meant to come to school early to learn it but the row delayed him. It had been about his father's boots. After breakfast she had found that there were holes in both his shoes. She held them up to the light which was on because the November morning was wet and dark.

'Merciful God, child,' she exclaimed, 'there's not a sole in your shoes. You can't go out in those.'

He was anxious to put them on and get out quickly, but everybody was in bad humour. He didn't dare to say anything. His sister was clearing part of the table and his brother Joseph, who worked, was rooting in drawers and corners and growling to everybody.

'Where the hell is the bicycle pump? You can't leave a thing out of your hand in this house.'

'I can wear my sandals,' Peter suggested.

'And it spilling out of the heavens—don't be daft, child.' Then she said, 'What am I to do at all?'

For a moment he hoped he might be kept at home. But his mother told his sister to root among the old boots in the press. Millie went out into the passage. On her way she trod on the cat, which meowed in intense agony.

'Blazes,' said his sister, 'that bloody cat.'

She came in with an old pair of his father's boots, and he was made try them on. They were too big.

'I'm not going out in those,' he said, 'I couldn't walk in them.'

But his mother and sister said they looked lovely. They went into unconvincing ecstasies. They looked perfect they said, each backing up the other. No one would notice.

'They look foolish,' he insisted, 'I won't wear them.'

'You'll do what you're told,' his sister said. They were all older than he and each in turn bullied him. But the idea of being made look ridiculous nerved him.

'I won't wear them,' he persisted. At that moment his brother Tom came in and Millie said quickly:

'Tom, speak to Peter—he's giving cheek to mammy.'

Tom was very fond of animals. 'I heard the cat,' he began,

looking threateningly at Peter who sometimes teased it. 'What were you doing to it?'

'Nothing,' Peter answered, 'Millie walked on it.' He tried to say something about the boots but the three of them told him to shut up and get to school. He could stand up to the others but he was afraid of Tom. So he had flopped along in the rain feeling miserable and hating it because people would be sure to know they were not his own boots.

The door opened and Mr O'Rourke came in. He was a huge man in tweeds. He was a fluent speaker of Irish and wore the gold *Fainne* in the lapel of his jacket. Both his wrists were covered with matted black hair.

'*Filidheact*' he roared and drew a leather from his hip pocket.

Then he shouted '*Dun do leabhar*' and hit the front desk a ferocious crack with the leather. Mr O'Rourke was an ardent Gael who gave his orders in Irish—even during English class. Someone had passed him up a poetry book and the rest closed theirs or turned them face downwards on their desks.

Mr O'Rourke, his eyes glaring terribly at the ceiling, from which plaster would fall in fine dust when the 3rd year students overhead tramped in or out, began to declaim:

'Did they dare, did they dare, to slay Eoghan Roe O'Neill?
Yes they slew with poison him they feared to meet with steel.'

He clenched his powerful fists and held them up rigidly before his chest.

'May God wither up their hearts, may their blood cease to flow!
May they walk in living death who poisoned Eoghan Roe!'

Then quite suddenly, in a business-like tone, he said, 'You—Daly.'

'Me sir?' said Daly, playing for time.

'Yes, you fool,' thundered Mr O'Rourke. 'You.'

Daly rose and repeated the first four lines. When he was half-way through the second stanza Mr O'Rourke bawled, 'Clancy.' Clancy rose and began to recite. They stood up and sat down as Mr O'Rourke commanded while he paced up and down the aisles between the seats. Twice he passed close to Peter. He stood for some time by Peter's desk bawling out names. The end of his

tweed jacket lay hypnotically along the edge of Peter's desk.
Cummins stumbled over the fourth verse and dried up completely.

'Line,' Mr O'Rourke bawled. Cummins, calmly pale, left his
desk and stepped out to the side of the class. Two more were sent
out. Mr O'Rourke walked up and down once more and stood
with his back to Peter. Looking at the desk at the very back he
suddenly bawled, 'Farrell.'

Peter's heart jerked. He rose to his feet. The back was still
towards him. He looked at it, a great mountain of tweed, with a
frayed collar over which the thick neck bulged in folds. He could
see the antennae of hair which sprouted from Mr O'Rourke's ears
and could smell the chalk-and-ink schoolmaster's smell of him.
It was a trick of Mr O'Rourke's to stand with his back to you and
then call your name. It made the shock more unnerving. Peter
gulped and was silent.

'Wail . . .' prompted Mr O'Rourke.

Peter said, 'Wail . . .'

Mr O'Rourke paced up to the head of the class once more.

'Wail—wail him through the island,' he said as he walked.
Then he turned around suddenly and said, 'Well, go on.'

'Wail, wail him through the island,' Peter said once more and
stopped.

'Weep,' hinted Mr O'Rourke.

He regarded Peter closely, his eyes narrowing.

'Weep,' said Peter, ransacking the darkness of his mind but
finding only emptiness.

'Weep, weep, weep,' Mr O'Rourke said, his voice rising.

Peter chanced his arm. He said, 'Wail, wail him through the
island weep, weep, weep.'

Mr O'Rourke stood up straight. His face conveyed at once
shock, surprise, pain.

'Get out to the line,' he roared, 'you thick lazy good-for-
nothing bloody imbecile. Tell him what it is, Clancy.' Clancy
dithered for a moment, closed his eyes and said:

'Sir—Wail, wail him through the island, weep, weep for our
pride
Would that on the battle field our gallant chief had died.'

Mr O'Rourke nodded with dangerous benevolence. As Peter
shuffled to the line the boots caught the iron upright of the desk
and made a great clamour. Mr O'Rourke gave him a cut with

the leather across the behind. 'Did you look at this, Farrell?' he asked.

Peter hesitated and said uncertainly, 'No, sir.'

'It wasn't worth your while, I suppose?'

'No sir. I hadn't time, sir.'

Just then the clock struck the hour. The class rose. Mr O'Rourke put the leather under his left armpit and crossed himself. '*In ainm an athar,*' he began. While they recited the *Hail Mary* Peter, unable to pray, stared at the leafless rain-soaked trees in the square and the serried rows of pale, prayerful faces. They sat down.

Mr O'Rourke turned to the class.

'Farrell hadn't time,' he announced pleasantly. Then he looked thunderously again at Peter. 'If it was an English penny dreadful about Public Schools or London crime you'd find time to read it quick enough, but when it's about the poor hunted martyrs and felons of your own unfortunate country by a patriot like Davis you've no time for it. You're the makings of a fine little Britisher.' With genuine pathos Mr O'Rourke then recited:

'The weapon of the Sassenach met him on his way
And he died at Cloch Uachter upon St Leonard's day.'

'That was the dear dying in any case, but if he died for the likes of you Farrell it was the dear bitter dying, no mistake about it.'

Peter said, 'I meant to learn it.'

'Hold out your hand. If I can't preach respect for the patriot dead into you, then honest to my stockings I'll beat respect into you. Hand.'

Peter held it out. He pulled his coat sleeve down over his wrist. The leather came down six times with a resounding impact. He tried to keep his thumb out of the way because if it hit you on the thumb it stung unbearably. But after four heavy slaps the hand began to curl of its own accord, curl and cripple like a little piece of tinfoil in a fire, until the thumb lay powerless across the palm, and the pain burned in his chest and constricted every muscle. But worse than the pain was the fear that he would cry. He was turning away when Mr O'Rourke said:

'Just a moment Farrell. I haven't finished.'

Mr O'Rourke gently took the fingers of Peter's hand, smoothing them out as he drew them once more into position. 'To teach you I'll take no defiance,' he said, in a friendly tone and raised the leather. Peter tried to hold his crippled hand steady.

He could not see properly going back to his desk and again the boots deceived him and he tripped and fell. As he picked himself up Mr O'Rourke, about to help him with another, though gentler, tap of the leather, stopped and exclaimed—

'Merciful God, child, where did you pick up the boots?'

The rest looked with curiosity. Clancy, who had twice excelled himself, tittered. Mr O'Rourke said, 'And what's the funny joke, Clancy?'

'Nothing, sir.'

'Soft as a woman's was your voice, O'Neill, bright was your eye,' recited Mr O'Rourke, in a voice as soft as a woman's, brightness in his eyes. 'Continue, Clancy.' But Clancy, the wind taken out of his sails, missed and went out to join the other three. Peter put his head on the desk, his raw hands tightly under his armpits, and nursed his wounds while the leather thudded patriotism and literature into the other, unmurmuring, four.

Swaine said nothing for a time. Now and then he glanced at Peter's face. He was staring straight at the book. His hands were tender, but the pain had ebbed away. Each still hid its rawness under a comfortably warm armpit.

'You got a heck of a hiding,' Swaine whispered at last. Peter said nothing.

'Ten is too much. He's not allowed to give you ten. If he gave me ten I'd bring my father up to him.'

Swaine was small, but his face was large and bony and when he took off his glasses sometimes to wipe them there was a small red weal on the bridge of his nose. Peter grunted and Swaine changed the subject.

'Tell us who owns the boots. They're not your own.'

'Yes they are,' Peter lied.

'Go on,' Swaine said, 'who owns them? Are they your brother's?'

'Shut up,' Peter menaced.

'Tell us,' Swaine persisted. 'I won't tell a soul. Honest.' He regarded Peter with sly curiosity. He whispered, 'I know they're not your own, but I wouldn't tell it. We sit beside one another. We're pals. You can tell me.'

'Curiosity killed the cat . . .' Peter said.

Swaine had the answer to that. With a sly grin he rejoined, 'Information made him fat.'

'If you must know,' Peter said, growing tired, 'they're my

father's. And if you tell anyone I'll break you up in little pieces. You just try breathing a word.'

Swaine sat back, satisfied.

Mr O'Rourke was saying the English used treachery when they poisoned Eoghan Roe. But what could be expected of the English except treachery?

'Hoof of the horse,' he quoted, 'horn of a bull, smile of a Saxon.' Three perils. Oliver Cromwell read his Bible while he quartered infants at their mother's breasts. People said let's forget all that. But we couldn't begin to forget it until we had our full freedom. Our own tongue, the sweet Gaelic *teanga*, must be restored once more as the spoken language of our race. It was the duty of all to study and work towards that end.

'And those of us who haven't time must be shown how to find the time. Isn't that a fact, Farrell?' he said. The class laughed. But the clock struck and Mr O'Rourke put the lament regretfully aside.

'Mathematics,' he announced, '*Ceimseata.*'

He had hoped it would continue to rain during lunch time so that they could stay in the classroom. But when the automatic bell clanged loudly and Mr O'Rourke opened the frosted window to look out, it had stopped. They trooped down the stairs. They pushed and jostled one another. Peter kept his hand for safety on the banisters. Going down the stairs made the boots seem larger. He made straight for the urinal and stayed there until the old brother whose duty it was for obscure moral reasons to patrol the place had passed through twice. The second time he said to him, 'My goodness boy, go out into the fresh air with your playmates. Shoo—boy—shoo,' and stared at Peter's retreating back with perplexity and suspicion.

Dillon came over as he was unwrapping his lunch and said, 'Did they dare, did they dare to slay Eoghan Roe O'Neill.'

'Oh, shut up,' Peter said.

Dillon linked his arm and said, 'You got an awful packet.' Then with genuine admiration he added, 'You took it super. He aimed for your wrist, too. Not a peek. You were wizard. Cripes. When I saw him getting ready for the last four I was praying you wouldn't cry.'

'I never cried yet,' Peter asserted.

'I know, but he lammed his hardest. You shouldn't have said you hadn't time.'

'He wouldn't make me cry,' Peter said grimly, 'not if he got up at 4 o'clock in the morning to try it.'

O'Rourke had lammed him all right, but there was no use trying to do anything about it. If he told his father and mother they would say he richly deserved it. It was his mother should have been lammed and not he.

'You were super anyway,' Dillon said warmly. They walked arm in arm. 'The Irish,' he added sagaciously, 'are an unfortunate bloody race. The father often says so.'

'Don't tell me,' Peter said with feeling.

'I mean, look at us. First Cromwell knocks hell out of us for being too Irish and then Rorky slaughters us for not being Irish enough.'

It was true. It was a pity they couldn't make up their minds.

Peter felt the comfort of Dillon's friendly arm. 'The boots are my father's,' he confided suddenly, 'my own had holes.' That made him feel better.

'What are you worrying about?' Dillon said, reassuringly. 'They look all right to me.'

When they were passing the row of water taps with the chained drinking vessels a voice cried, 'There's Farrell now.' A piece of crust hit Peter on the nose.

'Caesar sends his legate,' Dillon murmured. They gathered round. Clancy said, 'Hey, boys, Farrell is wearing someone else's boots.'

'Who lifted you into them?'

'Wait now,' said Clancy, 'let's see him walk. Go on—walk Farrell.'

Peter backed slowly towards the wall. He backed slowly until he felt the ridge of a downpipe hard against his back. Dillon came with him. 'Lay off, Clancy,' Dillon said. Swaine was there too. He was smiling, a small cat fat with information.

'Where did you get them, Farrell?'

'Pinched them.'

'Found them in an ashbin.'

'Make him walk,' Clancy insisted, 'let's see you walk, Farrell.'

'They're my own,' Peter said; 'they're a bit big—that's all.'

'Come on, Farrell—tell us whose they are.'

The grins grew wider.

Clancy said, 'They're his father's.'

'No, they're not,' Peter denied quickly.

'Yes, they are. He told Swaine. Didn't he, Swaine? He told you they were his father's.'

Swaine's grin froze. Peter fixed him with terrible eyes.

'Well, didn't he, Swaine? Go on, tell the chaps what he told you. Didn't he say they were his father's?'

Swaine edged backwards. 'That's right,' he said, 'he did.'

'Hey you chaps,' Clancy said, impatiently, 'let's make him walk. I vote . . .'

At that moment Peter, with a cry, sprang on Swaine. His fist smashed the glasses on Swaine's face. As they rolled over on the muddy ground, Swaine's nails tore his cheek. Peter saw the white terrified face under him. He beat at it in frenzy until it became covered with mud and blood.

'Cripes,' Clancy said in terror, 'look at Swaine's glasses. Haul him off lads.' They pulled him away and he lashed out at them with feet and hands. He lashed out awkwardly with the big boots which had caused the trouble. Swaine's nose and lips were bleeding so they took him over to the water tap and washed him. Dillon, who stood alone with Peter, brushed his clothes as best he could and fixed his collar and tie.

'You broke his glasses,' he said. 'There'll be a proper rucky if old Quinny sees him after lunch.'

'I don't care about Quinny.'

'I do then,' Dillon said fervently. 'He'll quarter us all in our mother's arms.'

They sat with their arms folded while Brother Quinlan in the high chair at the head of the class, gave religious instruction. Swaine kept his bruised face lowered. Without the glasses it had a bald, maimed look, as though his eyebrows, or a nose, or an eye, were missing. They had exchanged no words since the fight. Peter was aware of the boots. They were a defeat, something to be ashamed of. His mother only thought they would keep out the rain. She didn't understand that it would be better to have wet feet. People did not laugh at you because your feet were wet.

Brother Quinlan was speaking of our relationship to one another, of the boy to his neighbour and of the boy to his God. We communicated with one another, he said, by looks, gestures, speech. But these were surface contacts. They conveyed little of what went on in the mind, and nothing at all of the individual soul. Inside us, the greatest and the humblest of us, a whole world was locked. Even if we tried we could convey nothing of that interior world, that life which was nourished, as the poet had said, within the brain. In our interior life we stood without friend or ally—alone. In the darkness and silence of that interior and eternal world the immortal soul and its God were at all times face to face. No one else could peer into another's soul, neither our teacher, nor our father or mother, nor even our best friend. But God saw all. Every stray little thought which moved in that inaccessible world was as plain to Him as if it were thrown across the bright screen of a cinema. That was why we must be as careful to discipline our thoughts as our actions. Custody of the eyes, custody of the ears, but above all else custody . . .

Brother Quinlan let the sentence trail away and fixed his eyes on Swaine.

'You—boy,' he said in a voice which struggled to be patient, 'what are you doing with that handkerchief?'

Swaine's nose had started to bleed again. He said nothing. 'Stand up, boy,' Brother Quinlan commanded. He had glasses himself, which he wore during class on the tip of his nose. He was a big man too, and his head was bald in front, which made his large forehead appear even more massive. He stared over the glasses at Swaine.

'Come up here,' he said, screwing up his eyes, the fact that something was amiss with Swaine's face dawning gradually on him. Swaine came up to him, looking woebegone, still dabbing his nose with the handkerchief. Brother Quinlan contemplated the battered face for some time. He turned to the class.

'Whose handiwork is this?' he asked quietly. 'Stand up, the boy responsible for this.'

For a while nobody stirred. There was an uneasy stillness. Poker faces looked at the desks in front of them and waited. Peter looked around and saw Dillon gazing at him hopefully. After an unbearable moment feet shuffled and Peter stood up.

'I am, sir,' he said.

Brother Quinlan told Clancy to take Swaine out to the yard to bathe his nose. Then he spoke to the class about violence and what was worse, violence to a boy weaker than oneself. That was the resort of the bully and the scoundrel—physical violence—The Fist. At this Brother Quinlan held up his large bunched fist so that all might see it. Then with the other hand he indicated the picture of the Sacred Heart. Charity and Forbearance, he said, not vengeance and intolerance, those were qualities most dear to Our Blessed Lord.

'Are you not ashamed of yourself, Farrell? Do you think what you have done is a heroic or a creditable thing?'

'No, sir.'

'Then why did you do it, boy?'

Peter made no answer. It was no use making an answer. It was no use saying Swaine had squealed about the boots being his father's. Swaine's face was badly battered. But deep inside him Peter felt battered too. Brother Quinlan couldn't see your soul. He could see Swaine's face, though, when he fixed his glasses on him properly. Brother Quinlan took his silence for defiance.

'A blackguardly affair,' he pronounced, 'a low, cowardly assault. Hold out your hand.'

Peter hesitated. There was a limit. He hadn't meant not to learn the poetry and it wasn't his fault about the boots.

'He's been licked already, sir,' Dillon said. 'Mr O'Rourke gave him ten.'

'Mr O'Rourke is a discerning man,' said Brother Quinlan, 'but he doesn't seem to have given him half enough. Think of the state of that poor boy who has just gone out.'

Peter could think of nothing to say. He tried hard but there were no words there. Reluctantly he presented his hand. It was mudstained. Brother Quinlan looked at it with distaste. Then he proceeded to beat hell out of him, and charity and forbearance into him, in the same way as Mr O'Rourke earlier had hammered in patriotism and respect for Irish History.

It was raining again when he was going home. Usually there were three or four to go home with him, but this afternoon he went alone. He did not want them with him. He passed some shops and walked by the first small suburban gardens, with their sodden gravel paths and dripping gates. On the canal bridge a boy passed him pushing fuel in a pram. His feet were bare. The mud had splashed upwards in thick streaks to his knees. Peter kept his left hand under his coat. There was a blister on the ball of the thumb which ached now like a burn. Brother Quinlan did that. He probably didn't aim to hit the thumb as Mr O'Rourke always did, but his sight was so bad he had a rotten shot. The boots had got looser than they were earlier. He realized this when he saw Clancy with three or four others passing on the other side of the road. When Clancy waved and called to him, he backed auto-matically until he felt the parapet against his back.

'Hey Farrell,' they called. Then one of them, his head forward, his behind stuck out, began to waddle with grotesque movements up the road. The rest yelled to call Peter's attention. They indi-cated the mime. Come back if you like, they shouted. Peter waited until they had gone. Then he turned moodily down the bank of the canal. He walked with a stiff ungainly dignity, his mind not yet quite made up. Under the bridge the water was deep and narrow, and a raw wind which moaned in the high arch whipped coldly at his face. It might rain tomorrow and his shoes wouldn't be mended. If his mother thought the boots were all right God knows when his shoes would be mended. After a moment of indecision he took off the boots and dropped them, first one—and then the other—into the water.

There would be hell to pay when he came home without them. But there would be hell to pay anyway when Swaine's father sent around the note to say he had broken young Swaine's glasses. Like the time he broke the Cassidys' window. Half regretfully he stared at the silty water. He could see his father rising from the table to reach for the belt which hung behind the door. The out-look was frightening; but it was better to walk in your bare feet. It was better to walk without shoes and barefooted than to walk without dignity. He took off his stockings and stuffed them into his pocket. His heart sank as he felt the cold wet mud of the path on his bare feet.

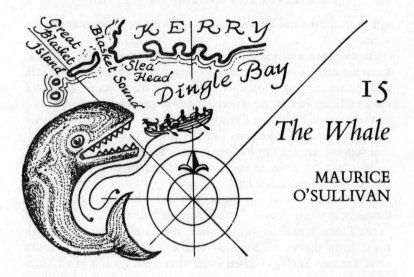

15

The Whale

MAURICE O'SULLIVAN

One fine October morning Michael Peg and I were in the house of Padrig O'Dala talking and conversing of the affairs of the world. After a while we wandered out into the yard. There was a light breeze from the east, rooks in plenty flying overhead and a fine settled look on the day.

'I wonder would you care to go west with me to the Inish?' said Padrig.

'Your soul to the devil, come!' said I with delight.

'Musha,' said he, looking out to the south-east. 'I have some fine new pots in the sea still and if I had them ashore they would serve me another year.'

'Faith, 'tis not better for us to be in,' said Michael.

'Get ready so,' said Padrig, and Michael and I went to get provisions for the journey.

I snatched a chunk of bread and hurried back. Michael was coming down the path, his cap on one side of his head, a pipe in his mouth and the smoke going up into the air, his shoulders stooping and the stones ringing from the nails on his boots.

'By God,' said he as he came down, 'it will make a great day.'

The curragh was afloat, each of us with his dog who knew well he was going hunting. As soon as the boat touched the water they leapt in, wagging their tails, their tongues out and barking to each other like any three men who would be talking together. We put our gear aboard and moved out along the coast of the island to the west.

As we were making Hill Head we got a nice breeze of wind from the east. When we were far enough out we drew up the sail, and out she moved swiftly. We were very comfortable, plenty of tobacco from Padrig, stretched out at our ease and Michael telling us the story of Robinson Crusoe. We listened intently, and so we were shortening the journey little by little.

'I suppose we are not half-way yet, Padrig,' said I.

'It is not far now, as soon as the Tearacht is visible beyond Black Head. Go on, Michael.'

The Tearacht came into sight. We had a beautiful view as we crossed the Great Sound. I could see the little white buildings up in the Tearacht and the shining white road built through the black rocks from the sea all the way to the lighthouse. To the south were the two Skelligs bathed in sunshine, the sea full of all kinds of sea-birds, the waves murmuring around us, Inish-vick-illaun and Inish-na-Bro growing bigger and bigger as we approached them, a group of sheep here and there on the top of Inish-na-Bro and others down in the steep, dizzy cliffs. How fearless they are, I thought, missing a good deal of the life of Robinson Crusoe on account of the beauty of the place and the depth of my thoughts.

Before long we saw the house on the Inish, its felt roof glittering in the sunlight and fine green fields around it. Farther to the west I saw a flock of goats and I thought of Robinson and of the goats he came across on an island just like this. Hundreds and thousands of birds were around, some of them flying through the air, others floating on the water, others settled on the rocks. I did not know what Michael was saying with all the thoughts that were running through my mind.

We were alongside the island now and I got the sweet smell of the fern, which grew to the height of a man. I was longing to go ashore. Padrig lifted his cap and looked around thinking. 'The first thing we had better do is to get the pots, for it is low tide now and we won't be long getting them if they are to be found at all. Then we can spend the day as we please!'

We rowed south to the bottom of the Carhach

'Take it easy now,' said Padrig, 'there's a pot here.'

I turned the curragh round on the pot, and he drew it up.

'Where does the next pot lie, Padrig?'

'We will go south to Moon Cave. There should be another there.'

We rowed on to the south till Padrig told us to stop. I looked in and saw a pot between me and the cave. We backed in. Padrig got hold of the cork and began to draw.

'Why is that cave called Moon Cave, Padrig?'

'I will tell you. Do you see the way its mouth is turned south-east? Well, there isn't another cave in the island that faces in that direction, and when the moon does be rising over Iveragh she throws a fine light straight into its mouth.'

We went on from one pot to another till at last we had five of them and I learned the name of each place from Padrig. We went west to Merchants' Gully, across the mouth of Bird Cove, all around the Thunder Rock, till we reached Gulls' Point. There we found another pot. Padrig was drawing it in, in a leisurely way, while he told us of the time when he was a child growing up in the Inish. Suddenly he stopped talking and looked up at a big high rock broken off from the island and about forty feet above the sea. I looked at him and could see that something was astonishing him.

'What do you see above?'

'I swear by the devil I see the queerest thing I ever saw.' He was peering intently.

'What is it?' said Michael.

'Don't you see the man seated above with a hard hat on him looking out to the Skellig?'

I looked up. There he was, clearly visible, his knees crossed. Nobody spoke. Who could it be? There was no one living in the Inish, and even if there were, how could he get out on that rock?

'Faith, Padrig, he is there without a doubt and, if so, he is not of this world.'

Michael looked at me and turned pale. I felt a shiver in my blood and a cold sweat came out on me. Then I thought I saw a mischievous look on Padrig. I began to think. At last I remembered my grandfather telling me once of a certain rock to be seen in the Inish called Micky the Pillar; which looked from the sea for all the world like a man in a hard hat. 'Your soul to the devil, isn't that Micky the Pillar?'

Padrig laughed. 'Upon my word, it gave the two of you a good fright.'

'Indeed,' said Michael, 'it is no laughing matter. I was terrified when I saw it.'

'You are not the first,' said Padrig, sitting on the thwart. 'But this won't do, my boys,' he said, putting out an oar. 'We are letting the day pass and doing nothing. We will go west through the Sound of Mantle Island and then make for the Strand.'

Suddenly Padrig stopped rowing and stood up: 'I swear by the devil those are tame geese in on the rocks,' said he pointing inshore.

'What would bring tame geese here?' said Michael.

'On my oath, a storm would,' said I.

He took in his oars and remained standing in the curragh till we were close upon them. 'Easy now,' said he, 'for fear they would fly.'

We counted nine of them. We backed her in, and Padrig had hardly stepped out of the boat when everyone of them leapt into the air and flew out into the bay between us and the Skellig. We kept our eyes on them until they settled on the water.

'Back her, back her,' shouted Padrig. 'Get outside them and we'll round them in before us.'

It was not long before we had rounded them in, ever and ever, until they swam into Yellow Beach and climbed up on to the rocks. Padrig leapt out after them but they all flew off again except one which he caught. 'Och, devil take them, they are long on the sea. Look,' said he, lifting up the goose, 'there's not a feather's weight in it.'

He crossed its two wings and threw it into the stern.

Off we went again, blind with sweat, till we had rounded in the other birds. At last we had six of them, and indeed the evening was now growing late for a star was to be seen here and there in the sky.

We went south through the Narrow Sound and then east alongside Inish-na-Bro. There was not a breath in the sky, glug-glag, glug-glag, from the falling tide out through the Sound to the south, sea-birds in thousands on the water, porpoises diving in and out between each other on the edges of the tide, a patch of mackerel here and there, a white path of foam in the wake of the curragh, a bright shining fish taking a leap into the air with the beauty of the evening.

When we were about twenty yards from the Laoch Reef I got a

very nasty smell: 'Poof, poof!' I cried for it was going through the back of my head.

'What's on you?'

'Och, don't you get the smell?'

I had hardly finished speaking when Michael and Padrig cried together: 'Poof, poof!'

At that moment I happened to glance out between me and Iveragh and about ten yards to the south I saw rings on the sea.

'The devil,' said I, 'what is that out there?'

Padrig gave a shout. 'Your soul to the devil, 'tis a whale, and it is from it we are getting the smell. Row, row as hard as you can and make for land.'

We pulled out, none of us speaking a word. There was nothing to be heard but the panting of the crew and the thud of the curragh leaping across a wave and the splash under her bow when she sent up a spurt of foam. We were pulling hard but had not gone far when the whale arose alongside the curragh—the biggest animal I ever saw, as long as a ship. You could see clearly its big blue gullet which could swallow three curraghs without any trouble. We were in great danger—out in the middle of the Great Sound, a couple of miles from land and that savage, ravenous, long-toothed monster up beside us, the way it had only to turn its head and swallow us up. I thought that at any moment we might be down in its belly. We were still pulling with all our strength, straining every sinew, the beast rolling along beside us, and from time to time giving us a side glance out of his two blue eyes.

'It will sink us if it moves across below the curragh,' said Padrig breathlessly. 'Row on, we are not far from land now, with the help of God.'

Our eyes and mouths were pouring sweat, our muscles bending with the strain, not a word spoken. I could hear the panting of the other two, the grating of the oars and the splashing of the beast through the water which kept sending spurts of foam into the curragh. And all the time the smell of its breath was affecting us. There was no escaping it.

'You had better not kill yourselves,' said Padrig, 'whatever it may do with us.'

He had scarcely spoken when the whale turned straight in towards the side of the boat.

'God have mercy on us, he has us now. Row! row!'

'What about throwing out one of the dogs to it?' said I.

'Arra, devil, row, or it will get you instead of the dog.'

By this time we were only ten yards from Black Head. We began to take heart when we found ourselves inshore, scraping the limpets from the rocks in our haste. We rowed east till we went into the Cave of the Palm. The whale came no farther. We stopped. We were unable to speak. Our breath was gone and our mouths wide open trying to fill our lungs. Padrig caught hold of a bottle of water that was in the stern and took a long pull out of it.

'Oh, God of Virtues,' said he, 'what a hacking day! The like of it never overtook me since I was born and God send it will not again. Arra, man,' said he to me, 'you were out of your mind that time, in the Great Sound, when you were for throwing the dog to the whale.'

'I wonder what it would have done if we had?' said Michael.

'You and the curragh would soon have been down its gullet.'

'Why do you say that, Padrig?'

'I will tell you. When the dog had pleased it, it would have been seeking another, though it would have only been a small morsel, and it would have set on the curragh and swallowed us all.'

'What was in my mind,' said I, 'was that it would spend a nice while eating it and then we could escape.'

'Och, that beast wouldn't have known it wasn't a fly it had swallowed.'

The sun had sunk in the west, the stars beginning to twinkle, wonderful colours spreading over the sky, a seal snoring here and there in the coves, rabbits over our heads among the clumps of thrift, sea-ravens standing on the rocks with their wings outspread.

'Let us move east in the name of God,' said Padrig, putting out his oars.

'It is often,' said Michael, 'that mockery comes to the bed of truth. Do you remember this morning when you let on that Micky the Pillar was a man from the other world? Wasn't it a fine burst of laughter you had at the two of us? But it is no thought of laughter you had back through the Great Sound.'

'Faith, I am thinking there was not a bit of fear on the two of ye.'

'The devil if there was much,' said I.

'No doubt, for ye did not know the way it was with that beast. If ye had known ye would have been in a yellow terror.'

'We can only die once,' said Michael, 'and if we had died in the Great Sound wouldn't we have been as well off?'

'And why, if you are so fearless, wouldn't you leap into the water now?'

'Och, that's talk without sense.'

'How so?'

'Because the day is appointed for us all.'

When we reached the quay there was nothing alive on the slip before us but a couple of water-hens picking mussels. When they saw us they flew out screaming over the pool.

the monster of Iniscathy

16

At The Foot Of The Rainbow

KEVIN DANAHER

Word went round the parish like wildfire. 'Levelling the old chimney in Seana-Mhuiris's bothan is what Mickeen was doing when the pickaxe hopped off an old canister, and if there was one sovereign in it there was fifty!' In actual fact, poor Mickeen had no such luck; there were six sovereigns and a few half-crowns in the mustard-tin he found. And by the time he had stood to all his well-wishers he had a hole in his week's wages as well as having said good-bye to his golden fortune. But was he believed? People are still wondering what he did with all his wealth, for by the time the tale had reached the end of the next parish, the fifty was five hundred—'the full of a three-legged pot, I'm telling you, and it all gold and silver coins!'

The hope of getting something for nothing is, no doubt, part of it, but there is more than this in the fascination which buried treasure holds for every one of us. It may be all the stories we heard as children. Of the crock of gold in the fort, and of the three men who went to dig it and saw their houses burning and had to run off home to save them. And of the cow's skin full of valuables that the monks buried in the field behind the blessed well when they heard that Cromwell's soldiers were coming; that one is guarded by the ghost of a black bull and no one can find it except a monk of the same order. And of the boy who turned a sod and found a treasure and marked the spot with a white stone, but when he returned there were hundreds of white stones in the field and no knowing which was the right one. And of the gold at the foot of the rainbow, which many of us set out to find, with spade on small shoulder, in our innocent childhood.

And, of course, of Paddy Ahern who dreamed three nights one after the other that he'd find a bag of money buried under Banogue Bridge, and walked the thirty miles there to look for it. He was poking around above on the bridge and below under the bridge until an old man of the place could contain his curiosity no longer. 'Is it any harm to ask what you are doing there, young fellow?'

'Such a thing, sir,' says Paddy, ''twas a dream I had three nights in a row that there was gold hidden near the bridge.'

'Wisha, you foolish boy, isn't it often I dreamt that there was the world of gold buried under a hawthorn bush in the haggard of one Paddy Ahern away in the west of the county! But sure dreams like that are all foolishness!'

'Well, I suppose they are, sir, and I suppose you're right, sir,' says my brave Paddy, not pretending anything, and away home with him, and there, sure enough, was the gold safely buried in an old crock. A while afterwards, with Paddy in ease and comfort, who should come the way but a poor scholar of great learning, and put up at Paddy's house for the night.

'That's a queer old crock you have,' says the poor scholar.

'And a lucky crock for me,' says Paddy.

'And queer old writing on it in the old Ogham characters,' says the poor scholar.

'Is that writing? 'Twas how I thought it was a sort of an ornament,' says Paddy.

'I'll read it for you,' says the poor scholar, 'although 'tis few could do as much. This is what it says—Twice as much on the other side.'

'My brave man,' says Paddy, 'and if that's true for you, you're the lucky man, for I'll halve it with you!'

Out they went and there was the other crock, twice as big and full to the brim with gold on the other side of the bush. So Paddy became the richest man in the parish, and the poor scholar bought a big house and started the finest school in the country. 'A fine story if it was true,' was the local verdict on this, and well might they doubt, for the same story is told in many countries.

But not all the stories of treasure are false. Precious objects and hoards are found from time to time, and more often than is usually believed. Take County Clare alone, for instance. Only twenty years ago a little girl driving the cows to the fields found a number of silver coins, and when her father dug in the place more than a thousand coins of about A.D. 1200 came to light. Not twenty years earlier a boy hunting rabbits in North Clare pulled a shining object out of a crevice in the crag, and it was later identified as a 'gorget', a gold collar of nearly two thousand years ago, more than a foot across and over half a pound in weight. Just over a hundred years ago when the railway from Limerick to Ennis was being laid, the workmen engaged in making a cutting came upon the greatest treasure find of recent times. Nobody knows exactly how great it was, for it was quickly divided up—the workmen grabbed up the objects and sold them off as best they could, and, as we may expect, got much less for them than they would have 'through the proper channels'. Certainly there were hundreds of objects there, mostly heavy gold bracelets, and the real value of the find, in today's money, would probably exceed £10,000. Three great finds in one county, and they could be echoed in almost every county. Cross the Shannon from Clare and you hear of the Roman silver found near Foynes or of that finest of all examples of the art of our Early Christian ancestors, the Ardagh Chalice found by a workman in the fort at Ardagh. Go north from Clare and you have Galway and the Moylough belt shrine found by a turf cutter during the war; on into County Mayo to hear of the astonishment of the worthy schoolmaster at Balla when one of the boys brought him a large gold 'fibula', a curved bar with a cup-like expansion at each end, something like a huge cuff link, about six inches across. All these, together with many hundreds of other gold and silver treasures, can be seen in the National Museum in Dublin to prove that so many tales of hidden wealth are true.

All very well, says the critic, but why all the noise about treasure that has been found? What about the hidden wealth that hasn't been found yet? A fair objection and a reasonable question. And some of it lies nearer than the foot of the rainbow. Under the gloomy cliffs of Comshingaun in County Waterford, so we are told, is hidden a riding boot full of guineas, stored away against a rainy day by the famous highwayman Crotty, who was betrayed and hanged before he could spend it; the only one who shared his secret was his wife, and she, poor thing, went berserk at the death of her husband and forgot all about the hidden hoard. Not very far away, near Killaughrim in County Wexford another notorious knight of the road hid his ill-gotten wealth and this has not yet been found in spite of long searching. Smugglers, too, had their hoards. A keg of gold is said to be hidden in the depths of a cave which can only be reached by boat between Ballybunion and Beal, and another cave, this one near Clogher in County Louth, has a similar cache.

All along the coasts of Ireland you can hear stories of pirates and wreckers, of lost ships and sunken treasure-chests. Take the case of the *Earl of Sandwich* on a voyage from America. This ship was found drifting off the Waterford coast, and when the crew of another ship boarded her they found that her captain, two sailors, two boys and a passenger and his wife and daughter had all been murdered in their sleep and the sea-cocks opened so that the ship would sink. The ship's papers showed that a great sum in silver dollars had been entrusted to the captain and this was missing. Meanwhile four strangers had aroused suspicion in Ballybrasil and New Ross, and soon the hue and cry was on and the men were taken; they were the cook, the boatswain and two seamen from the unlucky ship who had murdered the others and stolen the treasure. Later came soldiers from Duncannon Fort, searching along the shore, and they dug up two hundred and fifty bags of dollars which had been hidden in several different places around what has ever since been called Dollar Bay. The villains were tried in Dublin, executed, and their bodies hanged in chains on the Muglins rocks off Dalkey, but the story goes that not all the treasure was found and that bags of silver dollars still lie around Dollar Bay.

Then there was the *Golden Lion*, a Danish ship which ran aground in a storm near Kerry Head in the autumn of 1728. The people on board were saved and so was twenty thousand pounds worth of coin and bar silver which was stored at the house of the local landlord, Crosbie. But one dark night, shortly after this the Danish sentries were knocked down and tied up and the silver disappeared. The true facts never came to light and very little of the treasure was ever recovered. Local tradition still maintains that hoards of silver are hidden in the sandhills and along the cliffs.

'Sixty thousand ducats in coined money and as much again in gold and silver plate,' said the only survivor of the ship *Saint Mary of the Rose*, one of the Spanish Armada, which ran on a rock and went down in the Blasket Sound in the month of September 1588. The broken wreck still lies there; about seventy years ago some fishermen tangled their nets on a bronze gun and brought it ashore. Many other ships of the Armada struck on the west coast of Ireland, and each ship had a money-chest on board, with gold and silver coin to pay the sailors and soldiers and to buy stores and other necessaries. Few of these money-chests were ever recovered. One of them was brought ashore and hidden near Inver Bay in County Mayo, but the fellow who hid it was a half-wit who took the moon for his landmark and, unfortunately, the moon had moved by the time he got back to the treasure. Then there was the *Gran Grin* which went down on the north shore of Clew Bay, the *San Juan of Sicily* and two other ships which broke on Streedagh strand in County Sligo, the *Concepcion* which struck near Carna in Connemara, the *Balanzara* sunk near Moville in Inishowen, the *San Marcos* at Spanish Point in County Clare and the *Anunciada* burned and sunk off Carrigaholt in the same county. Some daring frogman may yet make a name and a fortune from one of these.

Inland the tales of treasure are not any less numerous. Pious benefactors in the days of peace gave sacred vessels, rich shrines, book-covers and vestments to many a church and abbey. Then came the impious freebooters of Queen Elizabeth and Oliver Cromwell, and often the monks or friars were able to hide the holy treasures away before fire and sword ended both their lives and that of their monasteries. We hear of this at Muckross Abbey near Killarney, at Claregalway and Abbeyknockmoy in County Galway, at Mourne Abbey, at Quin, at Holy Cross, at Rattoo, at Mainistir and at scores of other church, abbey and convent ruins. Then there are the castles besieged and taken in the long series of wars. We can be sure that the valuables and money were hidden away during the fight and that some of them were never found, the secret of their hiding-places dying with the slaughtered garrisons. Thus the story runs at Dunboy near Castletownbeare, at Glin and at Carrigogunnel in County Limerick, at Dunamase and Donegal and dozens of others.

Indeed there is hardly an ancient ruin, a burial mound or a stone circle without its story of hidden wealth. There is treasure at the bottom of lakes, guarded by fearsome serpents. There is gold under pillar-stones which turn into giants when treasure-hunters come to disturb it. There is the fairy hoard that turns to leaves or ashes in the pocket of the finder. And there still is, and always will be, the crock of gold at the foot of the rainbow.